Engaging stakeholders on projects

Engaging stakeholders on projects

How to harness people power

by
Elizabeth Harrin FAPM

Association for Project Management

Association for Project Management
Ibis House, Regent Park
Summerleys Road, Princes Risborough
Buckinghamshire
HP27 9LE

First published 2020

British Library Cataloguing in Publication Data is available.
Paperback ISBN: 978-1-913305-10-9
eISBN: 978-1-913305-11-6

Cover design by Fountainhead Creative Consultants
Typeset by RefineCatch Limited, Bungay, Suffolk
in 11/14pt Foundry Sans

Contents

Contents

Contents

Contents

Contents

List of figures

List of tables

Foreword

Projects exist to help stakeholders to maintain, grow or de-risk their business. It's an obvious statement to make and yet, there is an assumption that everyone knows how to do this well.

The project delivery world is full of assumptions. Assumptions that people who are asked to manage projects know how to lead, know how to build teams and have the discipline to get the job done. A big part of getting the job done lies in the ability to build relationships with stakeholders at the start of any new project and ensure that they remain effective through its life cycle such that the products that are delivered will produce the expected benefits. Project done, stakeholders happy, shut it down!

This is not as easy as it sounds.

Stakeholders have different motivations, interests, biases, pressures, opportunities, personalities and communication styles. They bring those things into the room with them, or else they only show themselves, when others bring theirs in too. Maintaining these relationships is a complex, messy business and if it is not managed properly then they can very quickly turn against a project manager who is left to wonder where it all went wrong.

Like the ability to inspire and motivate a team of people and provide certainty through planning, being able to manage stakeholders is a core competency for anyone involved in the delivery of everything. It can't be delegated or ignored. Indeed, it's such a core skill that project professionals are expected to excel at it and show others how to do it well.

To my knowledge no book has been written that's quite like this one in terms of the level of practical information that it provides. Elizabeth has built a successful career by putting herself in the service of others and this is clearly demonstrated in this comprehensive guide to relationship building and communication.

Reading through this book, I reflected back on my own project management career and how this would have really helped me through some challenging times.

In the early days and as a project manager by accident (like most people in our profession!), my knowledge of how to craft messages to gain buy-in was low. As was my level of influence and my resilience when I inevitably hit brick wall after brick wall.

I had been put in an environment where I didn't know the business as well as my stakeholders and didn't know the product as well as my project team. It took me a couple of months of coaching to fully grasp that it was my job not to understand these things like others did, but to understand them well enough to maintain relationships, ensure that progress was made and to ensure that risk was continually managed.

This meant having difficult conversations as well as praising the kinds of behaviours that I'd like to see repeated. It meant listening when I'd rather be talking, elevating others when I'd rather do something myself and building bridges when I'd rather let people do it for themselves.

These are all traits of project leaders, yet most people never achieve leadership status because they don't work hard at the things that don't come naturally to them or else assume (there's that word again) that because they have the word manager in their title and a couple of certificates to demonstrate their technical prowess then this automatically qualifies them as one.

It doesn't. The title of 'leader' isn't decided by the individual, it is decided by the people the person serves and those that have an interest in the project. Up until the early 2000s a command and control approach was still considered to be appropriate for many projects, and yet post-global financial crisis the world changed.

Managers that preferred authority over empathy were rejected by their staff and emotional maturity appeared on the list of project success factors for the first time. For those of you that have ever worked for a leader you'll know that as well as having strong technical capabilities (being able to ask the right questions at the right time), they were also high in emotional intelligence (EQ). And excelling at stakeholder management and engagement will require continual EQ.

The role that EQ plays in the success of project teams has been downplayed for far too long, but not any more. Emotional intelligence, the ability to recognise, manage and control one's emotions whilst building empathetic and judicious relationships is a skill that every manager (project or otherwise) needs to master in order to be successful.

It's covered at the start of the book in order to emphasise its importance and to remind you that if you can't stay in control of the way that you feel then you will lose influence, confidence and the trust from those around you very quickly.

Behaviours such as empathy, humility, vulnerability and courage are now valued as highly as the ability to build a work breakdown structure, run a risk workshop or write an informative project report. What will make you memorable

Foreword

to your stakeholders will be how you make them feel. This wasn't always the case, but in 2020 and beyond it is critical.

As with every good book you'll want to read it front to back to begin with, however, there is so much practical content here that you'll be jumping around it in no time! It's suitable for every project professional regardless of sector, country or area of expertise. Even with 20 years of experience myself, I still was able to take plenty of things away!

Managing stakeholders is a critical skill required by all managers and finally there is a book to help you to do just that.

Colin D Ellis
Melbourne
April 2020

Acknowledgments

I'd like to thank Patrick Mayfield and Tiago Dias for their thoughts on the early outline of this book; their comments helped make it better. The comments from anonymous reviewers were also very insightful.

Several of my colleagues took time out of their schedules to read and comment on the manuscript – special thanks go to Colin D. Ellis, Rick Morris and Peter Taylor.

My thanks go to Ruth Pearce, Kamil Mroz and Vladimir Polkovnikov who were part of an IPMA Young Crew panel with me. Our discussion helped shape the short section in the book on engagement during a crisis.

I would also like to thank Clare Georgy and the team at APM for their continued confidence and support for my work.

I'd like to close with the usual thanks to my family: my parents for their support (and proofreading) and Jon, Jack and Oliver, for again allowing me the time to engross myself in a subject long enough to produce a book and for supplying me with regular cups of tea.

About the author

Elizabeth Harrin, MA, FAPM, MBCS has been actively engaged in projects since 2000. She has worked in financial services and healthcare, in the UK and France, leading a range of projects from ERP implementations to compliance initiatives and IT-enabled business change.

Elizabeth is a PRINCE2, MSP and P3O Practitioner and holds the ITIL Foundation certificate. She is a Fellow of the Association for Project Management and a member of PMI. She holds degrees from the University of York and Roehampton University.

Elizabeth is director of Otobos Consultants Ltd, which does both copywriting for project management firms and support for individual project managers through training and mentoring.

She is the author of 5 other books about project management: *Shortcuts to Success: Project Management in the Real World* (which was a finalist in the Management Book of the Year Awards 2014 and now in its second edition), the PMI-best seller *Collaboration Tools for Project Managers*, *Communicating Change*, *Project Manager* and *Customer-Centric Project Management*.

Elizabeth is also the award-winning blogger behind *A Girl's Guide to Project Management*, which aims to help teams get work done. She is widely published on project management topics and has contributed to numerous websites and magazines.

Connect with Elizabeth
You can find Elizabeth online at GirlsGuidetoPM.com
or on Twitter @girlsguidetopm.

Facebook users can continue the conversation in the Project Management Café Facebook group: facebook.com/groups/projectmanagementcafe.

Preface

Engaging Stakeholders is a book for project delivery professionals. Whether you work at project, programme or portfolio level, you'll have stakeholders involved in your activities. This book will help address the challenges you face when dealing with project-driven change in organisations.

If you've been in or around project management a while, you will have heard about stakeholder management and noticed how the vocabulary has shifted to talk about stakeholder engagement instead. This is a good thing. But what does 'engagement' actually mean? What do I do to engage people? That's what I wanted this book to help with. I wrote it for project managers, change managers and team leaders who know they ought to be working with other people to effect change and deliver projects in their businesses, but don't know where to start.

The book steps through the process for thinking about who is going to be affected and how best to reach, engage and work with them. You'll learn how to use people power to minimise resistance to change, leading to higher project success rates and better morale across teams.

I wanted this book to answer the questions:

- Why do I need to involve people in my projects?
- What does engagement look like?
- What tools have I got available to do so?
- How do I actually do it?

The simple guiding principle for the book is that people deliver projects and we should focus on those people.

I have tried to write this book in an inclusive way, to reflect the work done at all levels of project and change management. However, 'project, programme and portfolio' becomes tedious to write out each time and tedious to read. At various points in this book I use 'project' as a shorthand for 'project, programme or portfolio'. Wherever it says 'project', please assume that I'm talking about ideas that can be extrapolated to all levels of change delivery within an organisation. Equally, 'project manager' can also be read to include 'programme manager' and 'portfolio manager'.

Preface

A book about stakeholders is necessarily a book about relationships at work and not all workplaces are the same. This book provides core concepts and techniques for making those workplace relationships positive, professional and effective.

However, you know your workplace better than I do. The guidance I give is designed to be adapted, tailored or modified to different situations. Consider the cultural nuances – whether they are to do with your corporate culture or the global nature of your team – and make whatever tweaks you feel necessary to tailor how you approach engaging your stakeholders.

How this book is organised

This book is organised into seven chapters.

Chapter 1 looks at stakeholder identification, sharing techniques for finding out who is a stakeholder on your project, how they are going to be involved. Stakeholder analysis and categorisation techniques are also covered.

Chapter 2 covers working successfully in the sociopolitical environment of your organisation through understanding how your project fits within the social system of your business and beyond. It looks at organisational influences on your project and planning in complex environments.

Chapter 3 is about engaging others, how to do it and how to tell if it is working. It's a practical chapter full of tips for how to engage people in your project work. There's also advice on working with sponsors, as a disengaged project sponsor can be a particular type of challenge for a project.

One of the most common techniques for engaging people is simply talking. Chapter 4 looks into facilitation and meetings, sharing advice you can use today to help boost the efficiency of your conversations in a meeting setting.

Chapter 5 is your guide to dealing with resistance to engagement. Some people aren't going to want, or have time, to engage with your project. This chapter draws on change management techniques to consider options for dealing with resistant stakeholders.

Chapter 6 covers conflict management and resolution. It looks at what causes conflict, common flashpoints, a process for managing conflict and techniques for resolving it, both face-to-face and in virtual teams.

Finally, Chapter 7 is a deeper dive into the skills that are beneficial for effective stakeholder engagement. So many interpersonal and technical skills come into play when engaging others, but I've picked out ten core skills and provided some ideas about how you can develop those to improve your practice.

At the end of most chapters you'll find action steps and key takeaways. The action steps are tasks for you to make your learning real. Reading a book about stakeholder engagement can only go some of the way to helping you improve your skills. Most of the improvement you'll see will come from doing the techniques, taking action and putting the information into practice at work.

Key takeaways are a list of summary points from the chapter. If you remember nothing else, remember those.

The book concludes with references and further reading. Here, you'll find a list of books that I have found useful over the years in my work on projects, programmes and portfolios of change. You may like to seek them out for more information on the concepts and techniques discussed in this book.

Introduction

The shift from 'management' to 'engagement'

For a long time, project management theory and practice focused on stakeholder management (when interpersonal relations were mentioned at all). Stakeholder 'management' implies that a stakeholder's behaviours and actions can be managed – predicted, planned, organised and controlled – which is both arrogant and inaccurate. Anyone who has ever tried to get anything done with a group of other people will realise that when humans are part of the equation, you can't expect things to go perfectly smoothly, as per the documented plan.

Management can also imply some kind of direct authority over the individuals. At work, you have a 'manager' who oversees and directs your tasks and who is above you in the hierarchical structure of the organisation.

Project managers often have to work with people over whom they have no direct authority. In complex matrix organisations, project professionals have to influence a wide range of people, most of whom will be outside of their direct sphere of control. Many of those will be people who are peers or more senior leaders in the organisational hierarchy. Project managers may nominally 'manage' the work, but in most situations you don't manage the people – not in the sense of being their line manager.

Project professionals and thought leaders in the field have been challenging the terminology of 'management' as it relates to stakeholder behaviour for some time now. The vocabulary and sentiment has gravitated towards engagement as a preferable model for building relationships and partnerships with the people who help you deliver the project.

Stakeholder engagement can be defined as:

> *The systematic identification, analysis, planning and implementation of actions designed to influence stakeholders.*

The definition of stakeholder engagement might look similar to what you would expect to see as part of your stakeholder management plan, and you would be right. Much of what was taught as stakeholder management is still useful. However, stakeholder engagement presents a significant change in how managers and teams think about the people involved in the project.

When stakeholders are to be managed, there's the risk that they are considered resources to be moved, used, shaped and controlled to our will. When you seek to manage and control behaviour, you don't let people have a say. They aren't a partner in the change. Rather, they are someone the change is done to.

Experience shows that successful projects are the ones where stakeholders want to take part, are supportive, are listened to and where they actively contribute. Project professionals want stakeholders on board, championing the changes we are delivering, understanding and living the changes and not simply tolerating our projects.

When managers choose terminology carefully and talk about engaging people on project delivery work, they elevate stakeholders to the role of valued partner, instead of simply a 'resource'. They become an equal, someone to work with instead of for.

Engagement forces us to think about people as individuals, with agency, preferences, interests and needs. It elevates our own behaviour so that we demonstrate leadership, motivation, coaching, influencing, teaching. We can show loyalty and personality. We are moved to appreciate their contribution and to help them gain meaning in the work they do.

It might seem like switching 'management' for 'engagement' is simply a case of using one business jargon term instead of another, but if you pause to reflect on what engagement means to you, you'll see it is a deeper and richer term to express the relationship project teams want to have with stakeholders.

Refocusing your efforts on stakeholder engagement will be incredibly powerful. If you do not currently use the language of engagement, your challenge begins today: stop talking about stakeholder management activities and switch to talking about engagement. Give it a week and see what difference you've managed to create in your stakeholder communities and project teams.

Why engage?

When you engage a stakeholder, you are helping them take part in the project. At a very basic level, project management is getting work done through other people. Managers want – and need – stakeholders to engage with them and the project. We want to encourage action-taking.

Effective engagement improves the chance of stakeholders doing what the team needs them to do on a project. When people are engaged, there is a higher likelihood that the project will achieve its objectives because the actions taken have had a positive impact on stakeholder behaviour.

Engagement serves two aims:

- It creates, uses and sustains positive interest in the work. Where stakeholders feel positively about projects and changes, engagement makes it easier for them to take part.
- It minimises or removes negative interest. Where stakeholders feel negatively about projects and changes, engagement helps understand their position and influence their perception.

There's no getting away from the fact that engagement is hard work. There are a lot of conversations to have, lots of discussion and talking to do. It is time consuming and that kind of relationship building doesn't come easily to some people. However, it doesn't have to be time consuming or difficult. Even project managers who think of themselves as introverted (like me) can do engagement. We'll see more about what engagement looks like and how to do it in Chapter 3.

You've picked up this book because you are interested in learning ways to get the best out of your stakeholder relationships to achieve your project, programme or portfolio objectives. You probably do not need to be told of the risks of not engaging stakeholders. You might have even lived through a couple of tricky situations where lack of support from stakeholders caused issues on your change programmes and seen some of the things below happen.

When enough time isn't spent on engagement:

- People don't pay attention to the change, resulting in rework or benefits that fail to be realised.
- People don't do what you need of them, so projects are constantly delayed.
- People don't complete their tasks on time, to the required level of quality, to the approved budget, or perhaps at all.
- People aren't committed to delivery so projects drift on and on without ever achieving anything the business considers valuable.

So how much time is enough time?

It depends.

You will no doubt work with people who are motivated, whom you trust to simply get on with the work. You know they'll follow through and deliver a good result. You choose to let those areas propel themselves forward – and they do.

You might leave other individuals or teams to get on with things because you have no choice. Their work isn't high priority and your time is scarce, or you aren't empowered to engage with them.

Another group might need more coaching through the work, more support or oversight.

As we go through the book we'll talk about how to assess the level of engagement stakeholders need to stay connected to the project work. Then you can judge what actions to take to get the best out of their efforts. Spoiler alert: even the most motivated, trustworthy colleagues still need some effort on your part to stay engaged. Everyone appreciates being acknowledged for their work.

Projects, programmes, portfolios and change are all easier when stakeholders are engaged. Who doesn't want their work life to be easier? The rest of this book provides the context and action steps for creating a culture where engagement is the norm for your own work, even if it isn't the norm for the organisation as a whole.

Are project team members stakeholders?

I consider the project manager, sponsor and team as stakeholders in the project. If the individuals feature on the project organisation chart, or in the RACI matrix, they are core (or internal) project team members.

Some organisations have a culture that considers the project team members and project manager as stakeholders. Some organisations separate their thinking about stakeholders from their thinking about how to successfully lead a team. Both approaches are valid. The important thing is that you know which approach applies to the way your organisation chooses to work. If there is no policy or formalised approach to answer the question of whether project team members are stakeholders or not, then consider that they are.

Table 0.1 shows one way of categorising project stakeholders into 'internal' and 'external' depending on how much they are involved in the day-to-day activities of the project.

Engaging and leading the core project team requires different types of activity to the way stakeholders are engaged outside of the project team. This book focuses on engaging stakeholders external to the core project team. Many of the techniques will be relevant for the way you wish to engage with the project team. Pick and choose what you think will work in your environment to get the best out of both the project team and your wider stakeholder community.

		Organisation	
		Internal	**External**
Core Project team	**Internal**	Project manager, project sponsor, business analyst, process owner, project team leads/workstream leads, subject matter experts engaged daily (or almost daily) on project work	Supplier project manager, third party resources providing skills/resources, subject matter experts engaged daily (or almost daily) on project work
	External	Customers of the project, end users, process users, subject matter experts providing ad hoc support e.g. legal/HR colleagues	Customers of the business, regulatory/professional bodies, consumer groups, unions

Table 0.1 Internal and external stakeholders

The life cycle of a stakeholder

Project professionals think of projects as having a life cycle: work begins, is carried out, is completed and delivered, hopefully creating something that adds value to the organisation.

Stakeholders also follow a life cycle. You start out not knowing who they are, you bring them into the project and involve them, then their involvement in the project comes to an end (even if they continue to be involved with the deliverable or change outside of the project).

There are four steps in the stakeholder life cycle, as shown in Figure 0.1. Before we dive into how you can effectively work with stakeholders, it helps to understand the journey stakeholders go through as they engage with the project.

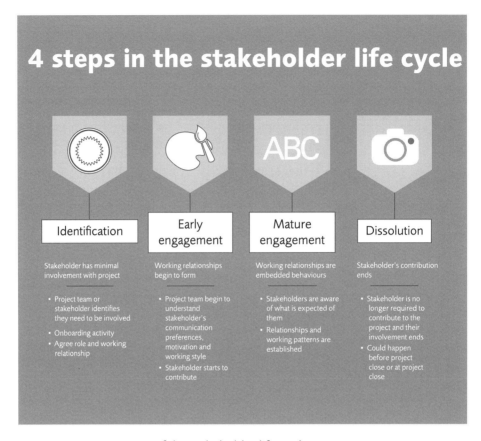

Figure 0.1 Four steps of the stakeholder life cycle

Stage 1: Identification

You identify the people who will be impacted or otherwise affected by the work you are doing. A stakeholder can also self-identify as someone who should be involved and put themselves forward for inclusion in the project work. This typically happens at the beginning of a project, but can happen at any time in the project or programme.

In this stage, you may not yet have any relationship with the stakeholder. You will bring them onboard, share the project's goals and objectives and establish what is required from the individual.

Stakeholder identification is discussed in more detail in Chapter 1.

Stage 2: Early engagement

At this stage, you are working out how best to interact with the stakeholder. You're establishing their communication preferences, learning about their management style and how they work.

It's the beginning of your relationship. This is the time to be making a good impression. It's also the time to begin to understand the people you are working with. You can't influence anyone if you can't see things from their point of view. You're finding out more about the environment they operate in, what matters to them and what motivates them.

Supportive stakeholders will embrace the opportunity to work with you and be on board with the project.

Unsupportive stakeholders will need more engagement activities to uncover their motivations and fully understand the sociopolitical context of their interactions with the project.

Someone could stay in the 'early engagement' period for some time until they are fully able to commit to the project.

Stage 3: Mature engagement

At this stage, your relationship, and the project's relationship, with the stakeholder is based on your past interactions. The relationship has existed for some time.

The stakeholder might be fully embedded in the team. If they aren't, the individual is at least aware of what's expected of them and their responsibilities to the project. They are aware of the project's goals, working patterns, expectations and rhythms.

Hopefully, they are fully contributing in the way you expect at this time. However, unsupportive stakeholders exist at all phases of your project and at all points of your interactions with them. You may come across individuals or groups with whom you have an established, but broadly negative, relationship.

Stage 4: Dissolution

Finally, the project comes to a planned or premature close and the stakeholder's interactions with the project also end.

Their position as a project stakeholder is wound up. For example, they sign off their project deliverables, or take delivery of the product.

An individual's involvement with the project may be dissolved before the project formally completes. For example, a lawyer with a single activity to review contracts at the start of the project will no longer need to be engaged in the project after that particular task is complete. Their involvement with the project can be wound up before the project finishes.

If you do need their involvement again, you may have to onboard them as a 'new' stakeholder, as the project may have moved on substantially since their last engagement with the team.

The dissolution of the stakeholders' relationship with the project is a little bit abstract and theoretical. Once the project is complete, they can't technically engage with it any longer.

However, stakeholders may have an ongoing relationship with the product, process, service or other output that the project delivered. You may personally continue to work with them on different projects or programmes, or as part of the wider portfolio. But the project itself is closed.

Project managers who build successful internal networks often find ways to stay in touch with key stakeholders even after a project has ended, because they know the relationship will help with future support or projects.

Key takeaways

- Project management thinking has moved beyond the language of 'managing' stakeholders to the more inclusive and collaborative language of 'engagement'.
- Effective engagement creates, uses and sustains positive interest in the work and minimises or removes negative interest. When people are engaged, there's a higher likelihood that the project will achieve its objectives because engagement (done well) creates a positive impact on stakeholder behaviour.
- Project team members should be considered stakeholders in the broadest sense, although you will engage with them more regularly and in a different way to your wider stakeholder community.
- Stakeholders go through a life cycle of engaging with the project, from identification and early engagement, through to mature engagement and dissolution as their project role ends.

1

Identifying stakeholders

One of the most crucial aspects of being able to engage people on your project is identifying the right people to engage with.

This chapter looks at the definition of stakeholders, how to identify who is a stakeholder in your work, stakeholder categorisation and tools for analysis.

Defining stakeholders

This book uses the *APM Body of Knowledge* definition of stakeholder:

> *Stakeholders are individuals or groups who have an interest or role in the project, programme or portfolio, or are impacted by it.*

Additionally, you may be dealing with stakeholders who feel they are involved or impacted . . . even if, by your assessment, they are not.

Stakeholders are often individuals, but can also be groups, such as a regulatory body or even a group of end users. In the case of a group, identify an individual who can be the nominated contact and representative for the project team. The project will benefit from having consistent representation from an individual on behalf of the group.

How to identify stakeholders

You can't engage people if you don't know who they are. The first step in any stakeholder engagement plan is identifying the right people.

There are a number of ways you can identify stakeholders who will have an interest in your project or be impacted by it. However, the bottom line is that you have to ask people. If you have been with your organisation for some time, you may know some of the key people who should be involved as stakeholders on the project. But in all other cases, you will need to rely on the knowledge of others in the organisation to help you identify your stakeholder groups.

Even if you *think* you know who should make up your stakeholder community, do not skip the identification step. There may be new joiners to the organisation, or subject matter experts you are not aware of who do need to be consulted. Take the time to do a full identification exercise and do not make assumptions based only on your knowledge.

Below are some techniques for identifying stakeholders. Use a couple of techniques, at least, to give you a solid foundation for your stakeholder identification exercise.

1. Stakeholder lists

Hold a workshop or team meeting with the objective of discussing and agreeing who needs to be included as stakeholders for this project, programme or portfolio activity.

Get the core project team together. At an early point in a project, this is likely to be you, the project sponsor, the programme manager (if the project is part of a programme) and perhaps a representative from the PMO.

Make sure the group understands the definition of a stakeholder and the scope of the project work.

Each person makes a list of the individuals or groups that could be considered stakeholders.

Compare the lists. You could do this in pairs, if you have enough people in the room. Talking to each other may prompt you to add more stakeholders to the list as you bounce ideas around.

Compile a master list of stakeholders, based on the individual lists.

2. Stakeholder segments

Again, get the core project team together, or the people who have some knowledge of the project at this point.

Provide them with a list of typical stakeholder segments or categories e.g. IT, compliance, marketing, PMO etc. A sample list of stakeholder segments is available in Appendix A. Remember to consider both stakeholders internal to the organisation and those external.

Use the list as a starting point for brainstorming who will need to be involved as a stakeholder in the project. Ask the team to identify the individuals who represent or fit into each segment. Ask them to identify missing segments or teams who should also be involved.

3. Ask known stakeholders

People who are already involved in the project will have a good idea of what the work entails. They will also know who is currently involved and who amongst their peers or contacts is not yet involved.

One of the most valuable ways to identify stakeholders is to ask the current known stakeholders who else should be involved in the project. Once the stakeholder has reached the early engagement stage of their life cycle, they will know enough about the project to be able to comment on who else should be brought into the team.

Another time to ask about who else should be involved is when preparing information for senior stakeholders. Ask them if they want you to discuss whatever you are preparing with other colleagues before they see the final version. They may direct you to individuals with useful opinions or data to share.

As your project evolves, so too does the group of people who need to be involved. Stakeholder identification is not a one-off exercise. As the project or programme manager, you should be constantly considering who else needs to know about your work. Every change, every new piece of functionality or organisational shift could result in new people needing to know about or contribute to the project. Ask yourself, your team and your current stakeholders: "Who else needs to know about this?"

Stay alert for points in the project when you will need to expand your stakeholder community. Equally, some stakeholders may drop out of your engagement activity as their role in the project comes to an end.

Categorisation of stakeholders

All stakeholders are not created equal. It's valuable to spend some time thinking about who your stakeholders are, what you need from them and what they need from you.

You need to consider where to spend your time. Liaising with stakeholders and working on engagement activities can take up a lot of time. While it is important work, you only have limited time during the working day and you want to make sure you are using that time wisely.

Categorising and analysing stakeholders helps ensure your efforts are spent on the relationships that will have the most impact on project success.

A simple way to categorise stakeholders is to consider them in terms of primary, secondary and interested groups.

Primary stakeholders

Primary stakeholders are those who form your core group of individuals (or groups) with whom the project will engage. These are the people who are fundamental to the success of the project and they will judge its success. They currently use the process or product that is being changed, or they are hands-on with what is being developed. This group will agree the overall scope of the project and have a big influence over requirements. They know they need to make time for the project. The project might be included in their strategic objectives as a department or team. They are invested in the outcome of the work and will use or benefit from the deliverable of the project, or the change and benefits created by the programme.

They may not feel positively about the project, but these individuals are the people you will be working with most regularly and who will have the most influence over the project.

You will prioritise spending time engaging and working with stakeholders in this group.

Secondary stakeholders

Secondary stakeholders are affected by the work of the project. They may have some input to the scope and they are aware of what challenges the work will bring.

However, they are not as influential. You may want to consult with them, but their opinions won't carry as much weight as those in your primary stakeholder group.

You will spend some of your time working with and engaging this group, but they won't get as much attention as your primary group.

Interested stakeholders

Interested stakeholders are those people who have no direct involvement in the project or process. They are not end users and they have no stake in the outcome. There is nothing the project will deliver that will impact them.

They still might feel they have a view to share. And that view could be useful and valid. However, this group will earn the least amount of your time.

Stakeholders can move between groups. Organisational structures change frequently, as do role descriptions and job holders. On a project or programme that runs for any length of time, be constantly on the lookout for people who are shifting between groups and therefore need more (or less) of your attention.

In addition, a potential relationship as a stakeholder could be as meaningful as a current relationship, for example, in the case of a prospective investor. They may not currently be a stakeholder, but their influence will be felt over the project as if they were one. Someone who is only 'interested' today could become a 'primary' stakeholder tomorrow.

Hidden stakeholders

Stakeholder identification and categorisation is all well and good, but you have to be really efficient not to miss anyone out.

Hidden stakeholders – those you fail to identify – can wield substantial power. And because you haven't considered them, your good intentions can leak away across the business.

You don't know what you don't know, so assume there are some stakeholders you haven't identified yet. Make stakeholder identification an ongoing activity. Here are some other things you can do to ensure your identification work includes as many individuals and groups as possible:

- Map data flows across the project and ensure data owners are on the stakeholder list.
- Map how processes interact and ensure process owners are on the stakeholder list.
- Look at the relationships stakeholders have with each other and other people who are not yet on the list.
- Look at who stakeholders rely on to complete their own work: this can uncover testing, quality, production, manufacturing, architecture teams etc. whose work sometimes happens behind the scenes.

Tools for gaining clarity on stakeholder involvement

At this point, you will have a list of individuals or groups who are stakeholders on the project. It's a list you will keep under constant review. While you may have done some simple categorisation, most projects and programmes will benefit from a deeper analysis of the stakeholders involved on the project.

All types of analysis have the end goal of helping you understand more about how a stakeholder will interact with the project. Will they be supportive? How do they like to work? Who influences them and who do they influence? This information helps you shape your engagement activities to be as effective as possible.

Sometimes, your analysis will be spending half an hour of thinking time with a coffee. Sometimes you will need to produce detailed stakeholder documentation. Typically, the larger and more complex the project, the more analysis it is beneficial to do. However, avoid getting stuck in analysis paralysis. You do eventually have to engage with these people. Creating documents about their opinions and behaviour simply delays the conversations you need to have.

There is no hard and fast rule about how much stakeholder analysis is appropriate for your project. You can always do more at a later point, so use your professional judgement to strike a balance between continuing your research and analysis and getting on with the project.

So how do you do the analysis? Let's look at some ways to analyse whether a stakeholder is likely to help or hinder your project.

Talk to stakeholders directly

The easiest way to find out how a stakeholder is feeling about the project is to ask them. Stakeholder analysis is not purely desk-based research. Set up some one-to-one meetings or informal interviews with the stakeholders you have identified and talk to them.

Ask them:

- What are you interested in, specifically, about this project?
- What do you hope will happen?
- What do you want to happen?
- What do you worry will happen?
- What do you want to stay the same?
- How can we best work together to get a great result?

People are more likely to open up about their aspirations and expectations for the project work if they are talking to you on an individual basis. However, you can also use focus groups, workshops or larger meetings to discuss stakeholder involvement and gauge their interest and influence over a project.

You can even use surveys, although these should be a last resort. They are best suited for capturing sentiment from a large group of people you may not otherwise be able to speak to, for example getting large scale feedback on a qualitative basis from employees or members of the public. Take care putting together any survey so it gives you data useful for making decisions and planning next steps.

Talk to colleagues about other stakeholders

Much of what you know about working with individual stakeholders will come from your personal experience. If you don't have personal experience, seek out people who do.

Talk to your manager, the PMO team, project managers who have worked with that individual before. Ask what the stakeholder is like to work with, what type of communication they respond well to and what else is going on in the sociopolitical context of the organisation that might be shaping their actions (more on this in Chapter 2).

This 'soft intelligence' is hugely useful but the opinions of others are inevitably viewed through their own lens. Take all the information onboard, but ultimately, form your own opinion of the individual and their potential impact on your work.

Stakeholder saliency

The stakeholder saliency model was proposed by Mitchell, Agle and Wood (1997). They define salience as:

> the degree to which managers give priority to competing stakeholder claims.

Their model looks at how vocal, visible and important a stakeholder is, allowing you to create a typology of stakeholders to whom you should pay attention.

There are three elements to consider, which together highlight the saliency of a stakeholder: in other words, how much priority you should give that stakeholder.

- **Legitimacy:** This is a measure of how much of a 'right' the stakeholder has to make requests of the project. This can be based on a contract, legal right, moral interest or some other claim to authority.
- **Power:** This is a measure of how much influence they have over actions and outcomes. Their power could derive from hierarchical status or prestige within

the organisation, money invested from a particular shareholder, ownership of resources required to successfully deliver the outcome, or similar.

- **Urgency:** This is a measure of how much immediate attention they demand and how unacceptable a delay in response/action is to the stakeholder. The expectation of urgency can result from some kind of ownership, previous experience where urgent action was taken that leads to continued expectations of comparable response times, a time-sensitive problem that creates exposure for the stakeholder, or similar.

Together, an assessment of these three elements can tell you how engaged a stakeholder is or will be in the work and how they could influence the project. This is useful information for tailoring your engagement activities and working out with whom to invest your time.

Figure 1.1 shows how power, legitimacy and urgency overlap to give stakeholders more or less saliency. Stakeholders that fall into areas where they have two or three elements of saliency are the ones to be most aware of and to spend the most time with.

Mitchell, Agle and Wood define these groups as follows:

Dominant stakeholders: This group has high power and also a legitimate influence over the project. An example would be the board of a company. The blend of power and legitimacy means they can act on their intentions, should they ever want to.

Dangerous stakeholders: This group has high power and also expects their needs to be met with a high degree of urgency. However, they have no legitimate claim over the project. The researchers point out that stakeholders in this group, for example pressure groups, can use coercive power and unlawful tactics to draw attention to their interest in the project.

Dependent stakeholders: This group has legitimacy and urgency but lacks real power to influence the direction of the project. An example would be the future process owner who will be responsible for running the activities resulting from the project's deliverables. They are 'dependent' because they depend on the power of others to generate action at this time.

Definitive stakeholders: This group meets all the criteria for saliency. They have high power in the situation, they have a legitimate claim over the project and they have a claim to urgency. Together this gives them an immediate mandate for priority action on the project. Typically, this situation occurs when a dominant stakeholder wants something done and gains urgency as a result.

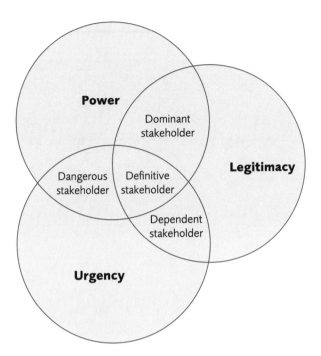

Figure 1.1 Stakeholder saliency

Source: Adapted from Mitchell, Agle and Wood (1997)

Stakeholders can move between the categories as the project and the situation evolve. Power, urgency and legitimacy can be lost and gained slowly over time, or in a moment.

Influence/Interest grid

Influence/Interest grids are simpler than saliency for assessing the impact a stakeholder will have on the project.

The grid works by considering the influence (or power over the project) and interest a stakeholder has in the project in a straightforward matrix as shown in Figure 1.2.

This matrix records:

- the relative power of a stakeholder to make changes on the project, either to the deliverables or the process;
- the degree of interest the stakeholder is expected to show about the project.

Engaging stakeholders on projects

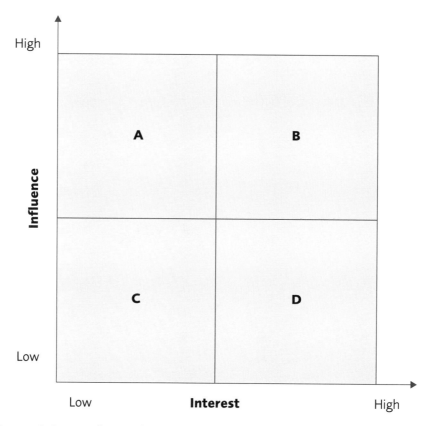

Figure 1.2 An influence/interest matrix

Engagement activities can then be planned based on the relative power and interest of stakeholders. As a simple example:

Box A: This is the group that you want to keep informed about your project. Let them know how things are going, but don't expect too much input back.

Box B: This group should be fully engaged in the project. Consult them, keep them in the picture, ask for their input and make sure they are on board.

Box C: Keep an eye on this group in case anyone moves from this group to another group by becoming more involved. Otherwise, let them know how things are going from time to time.

Box D: Ask these people for their input and identify their concerns, but be aware their voices are not as influential as others and manage your time and energy accordingly.

Positive/Negative influence

It's important to assess what kind of influence a stakeholder could have over the work.

Tempting as it is to assume that everyone will feel positively about your project, unfortunately that is rarely the case. Consider the likelihood to which the stakeholder will support the project.

A stakeholder with high power, high interest and low levels of support for the change could potentially be a blocker for the project. There's more on understanding and influencing stakeholders' support for change when they are not fully supportive in Chapter 5.

RACI matrix

Once you have completed your stakeholder analysis, another way to document how individuals will interact with each other and the project is to use a RACI matrix.

RACI (pronounced 'ray-see') is a way of categorising stakeholders to define their roles on a project. It forms part of the roles and responsibilities documentation. RACI stands for:

- **Responsible:** These people have responsibility for certain tasks. They are the 'creator' of the deliverable.
- **Accountable:** This is the person accountable for the job in hand who will give approval.
- **Consulted:** These people would like to know about the task. Their opinions are sought out before a decision or action.
- **Informed:** This group gets one-way communication to keep them up-to-date with progress and other messages after a decision or action.

Your organisation may use another category as well: **Supportive**, someone who can provide resources, information or will generally support you in getting the work done. This makes the acronym RASCI.

Remember that people can fall into several categories, as you can see in the example in Figure 1.3.

The RACI chart clearly explains the role each stakeholder will play on certain tasks in the project. It maps stakeholders (as individuals or groups) to activities, stating the level of involvement in the work expected from each.

Engaging stakeholders on projects

	Annie	Bill	Charly	Devi
Project planning	A	R	C	
Define requirements	C	R	R	C
Develop options	C	R	R	
Finalise solution	A	R	C	I
End user training	I	A		R

Figure 1.3 Example RACI matrix

The RACI matrix is useful because it:

- provides a starting point for communication plans. Stakeholders with different responsibilities will need different types or frequency of communication;
- flags which decisions are going to be made by consensus (where you have two or more people as 'Responsible') which may be a cause of conflict or delay;
- identifies who will be affected by changes to project process;
- clarifies for all stakeholders who has the final say and sign off of activities;
- helps identify which individuals may be overworked and have too much responsibility on the project;
- flags where stakeholders might be missing: a task without Consulted or Informed stakeholders might signify that a group has been overlooked.

The Praxis Framework explains that you create a RACI chart by:

> . . . combining two breakdown structures: the work breakdown structure with the organisational breakdown structure. If required, the work breakdown structure could be replaced with a product breakdown structure.[1]

---

[1] https://www.praxisframework.org/en/library/responsibility-assignment-matrix

In other words, create a table which lists the individual stakeholders or groups across the top and the core tasks down the side. You don't need to include every single project task. If it's helpful, create multiple RACI charts for different areas of the project.

In the matrix, populate the people who are Responsible first. Then add the Accountable individuals (only one per task), followed by the Consulted, Informed and Supportive (if using).

Draw on the expertise of your team to ensure that the information is balanced and correct. Share the draft RACI document with the relevant stakeholders and gain sign off for it, making any changes as required based on their feedback.

A large part of the value of a RACI chart comes from the discussion with stakeholders around creating it. The more you talk to stakeholders about what role you expect them to play, the greater clarity they will have about their input and the boundaries of their role.

At a project, programme or portfolio level, the distribution of responsibility forms a triangle, as you can see in Figure 1.4.

The distribution of roles across the project forms a triangle. There is only one person accountable for the project, programme or portfolio and they are at the top. You then have several people responsible for various elements of the work.

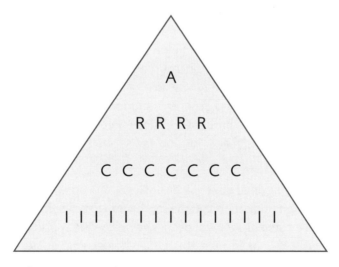

Figure 1.4 The RACI triangle

A larger group is consulted and provides input. An even larger group gets regular communications but is not active in any other way.

The value of analysis

Understanding more about your stakeholders and how they may interact with the project is important for several reasons.

- The way the project, programme, or portfolio is run will be shaped by the stakeholder landscape including, for example, the composition of project boards or steering groups, processes for decision making, communication approaches and risk management appetite and management.
- Vocal stakeholders may make decisions beyond their level of authority, which are likely to be challenged later by stakeholders with the appropriate legitimacy.
- Knowing who can influence others can help with change management: use influential experts to change the perceptions and behaviours of others.
- Disengaged stakeholders can cause problems and slow the project down.
- You can tailor your engagement efforts to the needs of stakeholder groups to have the most impact.
- You can manage your time effectively, prioritising interactions with the stakeholders who 'matter' most.

> During a project to deploy a new clinical system in a hospital, an IT project team found it difficult to gain buy in from consultant physicians. Stakeholder analysis allowed them to identify a senior doctor who was able to positively influence his colleagues and who was supportive of the new computer system. The project team brought him closer into the work. They used his influence with his peers to gain traction and support for the system rollout.

There's no denying that stakeholder analysis and documentation are great tools for project communication and the foundation for your engagement plans.

But you don't create engagement or change behaviour by filling in an influence and interest grid. You need more than stakeholder analysis to make people understand what you are trying to do.

You need actions. The actions that make up engagement and how to do them are covered in Chapter 3.

Stakeholder analysis is transitory

Stakeholder involvement in a project is analysed relative to other stakeholders. Stakeholder analysis using the saliency model or the influence/interest grid is useful only as it relates to this particular project. A stakeholder on one project may not have the same level of influence over another project because a different stakeholder on the second project has more influence.

When you are analysing the impact stakeholders will have on your project, look for the relative absence or presence of influence, interest, power, legitimacy and urgency.

Remember: none of this exists at a steady state. Stakeholder analysis is only as good as the day it was carried out.

Stakeholder influence, interest and power are transitory. They can increase and decrease at an alarming rate. People's priorities change and the attributes you use as an assessment tool are variable. Those attributes are also highly subjective, based on social and cultural constructs within your organisation and operating environment. While one stakeholder may believe themselves to have a legitimate ground for influencing a project, another stakeholder may disagree.

As a project delivery professional, part of your role is to try to keep up with the ever-changing stakeholder environment you find yourself working in by keeping

Note: Keep your analysis confidential

Your stakeholder grids, influence/interest matrix and other documentation include details that should be kept confidential. It is not appropriate to share your assessment of an individual's lack of interest in your project with the wider community in your business.

Anything you record about a stakeholder should be something you would be comfortable with saying to their face. However, if someone outside the project team finds your stakeholder assessment documentation in a shared computer folder or document sharing tool, they will be reading it without the context that you and your team have. Be mindful of how this information could appear to someone, if that was the only information they received about the stakeholder or the project.

Think about where you are storing your confidential stakeholder analysis documentation so that it is only accessible to people you trust to use it appropriately.

your relationships under constant scrutiny and review. There's more on working in a complex environment in Chapter 2.

Stakeholder analysis needs to be considered as a dynamic process that is constant throughout the life of the project, programme or portfolio. You will constantly be reviewing assumptions and changing your communication and engagement plans to respond to the current situation.

Stakeholder analysis works both ways

You are spending time working out who is impacted by the project, who should be a stakeholder and what their interest and influence levels are. You are considering how supportive they are, how credible they are and how you can work with them to influence the outcome of your project.

Your stakeholders are doing the same exercise about you.

Engagement works both ways: as you are assessing the impact stakeholders will have on a project, they are assessing the impact they think you will have on the project. They want to know that they are working with someone who is credible and professional.

Make sure they find out things that support the professional profile you wish to portray at work.

What will they find out about you?

Stakeholders will be looking to understand more about your experience and the kind of projects, programmes or portfolios you have been involved with in the past.

They will investigate your reputation, both in terms of your personal presence at work and your previous projects, with a view to finding out if you have a history of successful deliveries.

They will look at your LinkedIn profile. They will Google your name to find out about your past successes and whether your background supports what they think will make a good manager this time round, for the work you are currently doing.

Who will they find out from?

Savvy stakeholders will do their homework about who is leading their project. They will want to quickly gain confidence that you are a safe pair of hands, likely to deliver the project to the success criteria they have defined.

They will talk to your current manager. If you are new to the organisation, they may make enquiries to your past companies or clients, seeking out references.

They'll talk to people who have worked with you before, such as other stakeholders and your project team.

They'll also gain an impression from you. Your first impressions matter. If you want stakeholders to work with you and engage with the project, you need to be worthy of that investment.

There is no single thing you can do to create a professional personal profile that fills stakeholders with confidence. Building a reputation is a long-term activity. However, losing a reputation can happen quickly. Make sure that you consider what impression you are making in all your professional interactions, at all levels in the organisation. You might be surprised at what nuggets of information are shared about you between colleagues without your knowledge.

Action steps

- Choose a stakeholder analysis tool and carry out a review of the stakeholders on your project.
- Review and update your LinkedIn profile.
- Reflect on your personal profile at work and how you come across to others. Think about what steps you could take to create or reinforce the positive presence you wish to be in the organisation.

Key takeaways

- A stakeholder is an individual or group who has an interest or role in the project, programme or portfolio, or is impacted by it.
- Stakeholder analysis helps project teams understand the relative power, interest and influence of the individuals and groups and thus shapes how work is planned and delivered.
- Stakeholder analysis is transitory and only as relevant as the day it was produced. Understanding stakeholder relationships should be seen as a dynamic process throughout the life of the project, programme or portfolio.

2

Working where you are: Navigating sociopolitical complexity

Working in a project-based environment requires people to work together. Organisational constraints, like who is available to help and what tools you've got at your disposal, shape the environment you have to work in. When you understand the organisational context and the sociopolitical complexities of the environment, you can better drive and influence change.

This chapter looks at moving on from simple stakeholder analysis to understanding how the social system works in your organisation.

What is a social system?

A social system is the network of relationships and how they interact and influence each other as a whole.

It's a classic example of the whole being larger than the sum of its parts. Social systems understand that the connections between entities result in behaviour that you wouldn't (or couldn't) have predicted only by looking at the entities in isolation.

For example, while you might have a great relationship with Person X, when Person Y is added to the team, the dynamic changes: that's the social system at play.

To fully understand the social system for your project, you need to move beyond the influence/interest grid and individual stakeholder analysis. Instead, it's important to look at how all the parts fit together to create a project ecosystem.

Social network diagrams

Social network diagrams, also called soft systems diagrams, are a way of visually displaying the relationships and connections between stakeholders and influencers on a project.

Engaging stakeholders on projects

The social network diagram can be a good way to highlight how stakeholders are connected and the 'flow' of influence around the project ecosystem. They can help the team understand who needs to be engaged and how best to achieve that. The information in the diagram can also be a source of behaviour-based risk and can feed into your risk identification exercises.

However, social network diagrams start to look messy when you include lots of people on them. The more boxes and lines you have, the harder they are to read – beyond the simple appreciation that this project has a web of human interaction.

The relationships are likely to be less complex on projects with only a few stakeholders, making the need for a network diagram less relevant.

Use a social network diagram if you feel it adds value to your understanding of the interactions between people on the project. You might find it easier to quickly create a rough version with sticky notes on a large piece of paper before transferring it to a mind mapping tool.

You can shape the social system for your project. For example, define clear roles and responsibilities for team members so everyone knows the contribution they make. Co-create and sustain a coherent project culture with the project sponsor to reduce potential conflict and resistance to change.

It is not always easy to define these things because the social system for your project is complex and evolving. Some challenges include:

- Multiple organisations working together on a project, either in partnership or in a client/supplier relationship. This brings different organisational cultures and social systems to the wider team.
- Tenure of the individuals within the network. Research by Alia Crocker and colleagues[2] shows that it can take three to five years for a new starter to replicate the connections that a high performer has within the network.
- Perceptions of priorities may differ between stakeholders.
- Cultural norms and expectations.

There is also the challenge that the social network for your project is not the only network in the organisation. And the multiple networks within the company do not mirror the organisational hierarchy or formal reporting structure.

---

[2] https://hbr.org/2018/05/how-to-make-sure-agile-teams-can-work-together accessed 29 February 2020.

The research from Crocker et al also shows that 20–35 per cent of valuable collaborations come from only 3–5 per cent of employees. Your project network is likely to rely on some core players within the organisation who are also critical to other projects. Understanding the interdependencies between 'your' social network and that of other projects can help you manage the workload and project risk more effectively. For example, what would happen if another project was suddenly cut from the portfolio? The ripple effect could impact your project too.

Where project complexity stems from human interaction, you get power struggles, miscommunication and conflict. As a project leader, you then have to spend a lot of time and energy resolving those challenges. The greater your understanding of the social system in which your project operates, the greater your chance of being able to spot challenges before they become serious issues for the project.

The project ecosystem you work within is complex. It adapts to environmental changes, for example, stakeholders leaving or joining the organisation. Informal stakeholder power manifests itself as a self-organising element of the system.

Jonathan Sapir's book, *Thriving at the Edge of Chaos*, talks about complex adaptive systems, an example of which would be a complex project within an organisation. To best work within a complex project ecosystem, he advises focusing on recognising the way information flows and how people work with each other. This will get you to a deeper level of understanding than if you focus on the simple elements of cause and effect.

Stay curious; keep asking 'why?'

What do positive project cultures look like?

You may have had the unfortunate experience of working in an organisation where the culture feels toxic. It feels unpleasant because you're never quite sure who you can trust, or whether your opinion is wanted or respected.

Your goal as a project leader is to create the opposite: an environment where everyone can do their best work and is supported to do so in a culture that feels inclusive, respectful, dynamic and fun.

Engaging stakeholders on projects

In his book, *Culture Fix: How to Create a Great Place to Work*, Colin D. Ellis writes:

> Culture is the thing that gets people out of bed in the morning and is often the last thing people think of before they go to bed at night. It brings people together and tears them apart. It generates optimism and can make or break a weekend or holiday.

At its heart, the project culture is how you feel and how you behave at work, doing your tasks and interacting with your team. You spend a lot of time at work. Projects can be quite intense environments. It's worth putting thought and action into building a culture that people want to be part of. If nothing else, it makes it easier to secure resources as people will want to work with you.

Ellis describes six pillars of workplace culture in his book:

- personality and communication;
- vision;
- values;
- behaviour;
- collaboration; and
- innovation.

That's a lot to consider and would require more space than this book has available for the topic. However, those are the core themes to think about when you turn up to work tomorrow.

Ultimately, the positive project culture you want to see starts with you. As the project leader, you co-create the culture with the project sponsor. And together, you sustain it as new people join the project team and others leave. How can you foster an environment where those six pillars of workplace culture are baked into what you do every day?

Project culture fits within the existing organisational culture, as well as the wider cultural norms for your industry and geographic location or societal culture. It can be difficult to create a project culture that is substantively different from the current organisational culture. If you feel that the organisational culture does not lend itself to creating an environment for project success, that's a conversation to have with the management team.

The effects of working in a positive environment are far-reaching. People are happier to turn up to work and enjoy working when they get there. There is a positive effect on staff morale. A positive culture also contributes to removing potential conflict and resistance to change.

There is no single recipe for what your project culture should look like, but if you want to create or maintain a positive culture, you have to put some effort in. Do what you say you are going to do. Model the behaviours you wish to see. Praise where it is due and (gently) call out behaviour that doesn't fit with your culture expectations.

Emotional intelligence

Creating a positive project culture, and operating successfully within your project's social system, relies on you being able to demonstrate emotional intelligence. Emotional intelligence (EQ) involves allowing yourself to use emotions in your thinking, understanding emotions and their meaning in others, and having and showing empathy.

Anthony Mersino writes in his book, *Emotional Intelligence for Project Managers*, "You cannot make up for soft skills with hard work."

To be able to understand organisational complexity, you need to appreciate that it is predicated on the ability to make connections, build relationships, join the dots, use emotional intelligence and be personally and socially aware. To some people, using these soft skills comes easily. Others need to work more consciously to get the same results.

Mersino defines emotional intelligence as:

> *knowing and managing our own emotions and those of others for improved performance.*

There have been several frameworks for emotional intelligence published over the years, as research into this area has developed. Mersino's own framework for emotional intelligence in project management draws on the work of Daniel Goleman.

In Table 2.1 you can see Mersino's framework, along with my own interpretation of how these competencies relate to project delivery in complex project environments.

This section has not gone deeply into emotional intelligence, but rest assured it is something you can improve and develop. There are resources to help in Chapter 7 and the references at the back of the book.

	Anthony Mersino's Emotional Intelligence Framework for Project Management	Application to complex project environments
1	**Self-awareness** • Emotional self-awareness • Accurate self-assessment • Self-confidence	Being able to identify your emotions and how they influence your ability to do your job. Understanding what drives your levels of self-confidence and having the resilience to deal with a bad day.
2	**Self-management** • Self-control	Being able to remain calm and patient, even when the project seems to be unravelling before your very eyes.
3	**Social awareness** • Empathy • Organisational awareness • Seeing others clearly • Emotional boundaries	Being able to recognise and interpret the emotions of others and understand the impact of these on the current project situation. Recognising when you feel under emotional pressure to say 'yes' when the answer should be 'no' and recognising when you are putting that pressure on others.
4	**Relationship management** • Stakeholder relationships • Developing others • Truth telling	Understanding strengths and weaknesses in order to best build a team for project delivery. Being honest in all project dealings, but doing so in a responsible way.
5	**Team leadership** • Communications • Conflict management • Inspirational leadership	Being able to help a team navigate complexity through individual and group interactions that support the positive culture you've created.

Table 2.1 Emotional intelligence framework for project management

Source: Adapted from Mersino, 2013

People don't always react in the way you expect them to. When you expect a certain result after you engage with someone and don't get that response, you can feel disorientated. If that happens, reflect on your motivations and what might be motivating them. You didn't have all the information before going into the discussion. That's OK, you can't possibly know everything, all the time. What will you do differently next time to learn from this situation?

The role of politics

Organisational politics exists in all organisations. It's simply how formal and informal power structures work together to get things done and make decisions. In her book, *Project Politics*, Nita Martin describes it like this:

> *Politics is defined as the process by which decisions are made by people. . . . The term 'politics' is often used in a project environment, where it also refers to the way in which projects are governed. On projects, both the formal and informal processes and the situations which arise are considered part of the politics.*

Organisational politics helps you understand the alliances between stakeholders, the hidden and explicit agendas of influencers on the project and how an individual's personal objectives align with project objectives, if, indeed, they do.

However, you might not be aware of the politics that influence your project. Lack of awareness can create issues. As politics threads through the way decisions are made and how influence works, it is important to understand how people work together to deliver a successful result.

The more you understand about the personalities and relationships affecting your project, the greater the chance of being able to operate successfully within that framework. You'll be able to choose the best engagement and communication approaches when you understand how a stakeholder is motivated by the network of social relationships and their personal interests.

Politics and personality can have a greater influence on project success than project management processes. A team committed to delivering something awesome can often achieve that exact result with a minimum of formal project management structure.

Project professionals can't escape the fact that projects are done by people. It's the interactions between people that make the work happen (or not). Even if you don't agree with some of the political posturing on your project, understanding that it is there can reduce your stress levels because you can stop asking yourself the frustrating question: "Why did that happen?"

Uncovering the social system for your project

How do you go about understanding the social system for your project? If you can't see them, how can you cut down the time it takes to work out the power dynamics?

It's often not possible to ask other people to explain the project's social system to you. They might not understand the term, or they might not want, or be able, to articulate the relationships and political structures involved.

Understanding the soft power and influencer networks within an organisation comes with time. Once you've been in the business for a while, you'll pick up the subtle clues about who is influenced by whom, or why so-and-so always gets involved in that kind of decision.

Unfortunately, project delivery professionals often don't have the luxury of time. Contractors, new starters and even those with only a few years in the business, will not have worked in an organisation for long enough to have absorbed and internalised these social structures. So how can you quickly pick up what you need to know?

Every organisation is different, so it's impossible to give you a step-by-step recipe for uncovering the social system your project operates in. Here are some tactics to consider: pick and choose the ones you think will be most relevant for your environment.

1. Review the team structure

The structure of the project team shapes the influence the project manager and sponsor have over the project resources. It's the first thing to understand about the social system you find yourself in.

There are three organisational structures in project environments: functional, projectised and matrix.

Matrix structures are very common in project-driven organisations. The term 'matrix' is derived from the fact that projects, programmes and portfolios use resources from teams who also run business-as-usual activities. There is a crossover between the individuals working on a project and the individuals running the day-to-day operations of the business. The points at which projects and BAU work intersect, as shown in Figure 2.1, can often be a source of complexity and challenge for the individual and the project manager, due to competing priorities for their time and split responsibilities between different hierarchical managers.

Matrix structures provide lots of flexibility for an organisation and a project team. If you find you need a different type of resource, you can find an individual from across the business who can fill that need. It's a relatively easy job to onboard them into the team in a way that isn't as easy when the team directly reports to the project manager.

Table 2.2 shows different team structures and advantages and disadvantages of each. In real life, there is more fluidity between the structures. Organisations tend to operate on a continuum of authority and project structure, as outlined in Figure 2.2.

If you have high authority over the project team, you also have more influence. On the other hand, if your project structure is a weaker or balanced matrix, your position carries less importance for the team. You'll need to spend more time influencing and negotiating to secure resources and support for delivery.

However, in complex project environments even the organisational continuum doesn't always hold true. You might have some resources seconded to the project on a full-time basis, others drawn from the matrix in the organisation and project support staff being borrowed from the PMO, which is also supporting other initiatives.

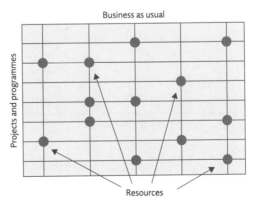

Figure 2.1 The intersections between individuals working on projects and business as usual work in a matrix structure

Source: Adapted from the Praxis Framework

Structure	Advantages	Disadvantages
Functional: Project activities are carried out in one department	Easy access to resources and decision making from the functional manager.	Low levels of authority for the project manager means this is more of a work coordination role than 'true' project management.
Projectised: Project team members report to the project manager	Project manager has full authority and control over resources.	Project manager has to carry out line management responsibilities which can be time-consuming and not part of the core skill set.
Weak Matrix: Project is delivered by people working in different departments	Managers can control the tasks their team members work on . . . but there isn't much going for this way of organising work for projects.	No single point of accountability. Individuals report to their team manager, not a project manager. There is no project manager.
Balanced Matrix: Project manager is appointed in one department to coordinate the work of other department resources	A project manager is in post to oversee delivery. An efficient way to organise work as subject matter experts can be affiliated to more than one project.	Team may not feel the chosen project manager adequately represents their interests as they come from another department. Potential for conflict between the needs of the department and the needs of the project. Project manager does not have control over the resources as they still work for the department manager.
Strong Matrix: Resources are seconded to the project team while remaining under 'formal' line management from their home department	Project manager has more control over resources. Resources have time to dedicate to the project with no conflict with BAU work.	Functional managers may prevent their 'best' resources from being on the project team for fear of losing them.

Table 2.2 Different team structures

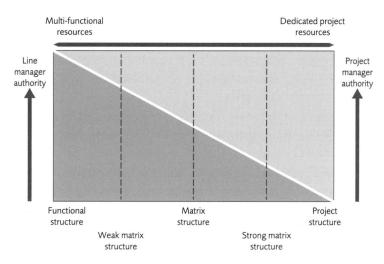

Figure 2.2 The organisational continuum of authority and project structure

2. Use your network

The second way to uncover more about the social system for your project is to ask questions of your network.

Your internal trusted advisors – your manager, your mentor, your project sponsor, a PMO leader – can be a huge source of information about the sociopolitical complexity of an organisation, especially if they have worked in the business for some time.

Ask them to fill you in on how decisions are made and what they see as the informal power structures in the enterprise. Ask who could influence whom, who should be included in the conversations and what their reaction might be if you took a certain action.

These conversations form a way to gather 'soft intelligence': emotional feedback about the context, people and situational aspects relating to your project.

3. Talk to stakeholders

You can learn a lot about how an individual operates and how they fit within the social structure of the team simply by spending time with them. Ask what problems they have and try to understand the challenges their area is facing.

Face time with stakeholders also helps you understand their working preferences. Are they detailed people? Do they need data to make decisions or do they primarily go from gut feel? It's OK to ask them their management style and preferences so you can better tailor your interactions to serve them more effectively.

Some businesses routinely offer employees the option to take personality-style questionnaires like the Enneagram or Myers-Briggs Type Indicator. The language of these surveys can become embedded in the jargon of the organisation. For example, one team I worked with had the results of their personality test shared in public view on their desks so that their colleagues had a visual reminder of how best to interact with them.

All of this can give you insights into the motivation driving stakeholders' behaviour.

4. Think strategically

Your project is not the only thing happening in the organisation. Read the industry press. Look at the published business annual reports for the past couple of years. Understand the context your business operates in. Talk to other project leaders and find out what their projects are doing, even if they have no overlap with your work. Be curious.

Build your business acumen as quickly as you can by finding out how the company makes money, gains and keeps customers and defines strategy. Think bigger than your project. Your stakeholders already think that way.

The journey to project engagement

The team structure influences the sociopolitical environment. The people within the structure are also influencers. It's time to look again at the individual stakeholders who make up the social network for your project.

Part of your initial stakeholder analysis, as discussed in Chapter 1, was to assess positive and negative influence from stakeholders.

Now it's time to go beyond that. In particular, it's essential to understand the journey stakeholders need to go on to provide the level of support required for the project to succeed.

First, let's acknowledge that it isn't necessary for every stakeholder to be whooping from the rooftops about your project. The level of engagement required from some stakeholders may simply need to be that they are *not* actively opposing the change you are delivering. That may be adequate. You would, however, expect more positive engagement from core stakeholders who will be substantively affected by the project.

There's a sliding scale of stakeholder engagement that stretches from openly hostile to proactive leadership. You can create your own scale using terminology that resonates within your organisation, but here's a simple framework to get started with.

Resistant stakeholders

These are people who are resistant to the change you want to introduce. They may silently or vocally oppose your work. They can go out of their way to be unhelpful or to talk negatively to others about the project.

Indifferent stakeholders

Indifferent stakeholders don't have much of an opinion about your project. They may not feel it has anything to do with them. They're not openly hostile but they aren't leaping to volunteer at meetings either.

Indifferent stakeholders can evolve in either direction, so don't write them off completely.

Supportive stakeholders

These are individuals who are happy to be identified as supportive of the project. They turn up to meetings and make small contributions. You can ask them for help.

Proactive stakeholders

These are your advocates. They are the people who are fully supportive of the project's mission. They champion the project in their interactions with other people. You can rely on them to complete their actions and to help you navigate sociopolitical complexities. They deal with roadblocks proactively and then let you know what they've done.

For each individual or stakeholder group, plot what you believe to be their current engagement level on a table or graph like the example in Figure 2.3. Also note where you want them to end up on their stakeholder journey,

		Current and desired engagement level			
		Resistant	Indifferent	Supportive	Proactive
Stakeholder	Product owner		⟶		→
	Scrum master			⟶	→
	UX designer			→	
	Compliance manager		→		

Figure 2.3 Example of stakeholder engagement modelling

acknowledging that different types of stakeholders are required to engage to different levels.

As you work through your stakeholder communities, you'll be able to see which groups have the furthest to go. Then you can plan your communication and engagement activities accordingly.

Stakeholders are not fixed in their level of engagement. A resister can be influenced and engaged to become someone who fully supports the project. Someone who is proactive in their engagement can become disengaged over time.

Any analysis you do of stakeholders is transient and based on where they are at the moment. You should always keep in mind that analysis should be revisited regularly and that we're talking about humans with agency, not data points.

Understand their level of engagement in the project today. How are they feeling about the project? Or, if the whole project seems like too big an item for where you are right now, think about how they feel about the next task, phase or step of the project.

It can be useful to think about mentally stepping into their shoes and trying to fully understand what is motivating their actions and behaviours.

It's often too much of a leap to move someone from resistant to proactive with a single action. Think about what you can do to move each individual along their personal engagement journey so they reach the level you think they should be at to effectively support the project.

Below are some examples of what you could do to understand and engage with stakeholders at common engagement levels.

1. They are resistant and you need them to be indifferent

Resistance often stems from wanting to defend the status quo. The Five Whys exercise is useful to dig into why a person feels like that. One reason is because they don't see that there is a problem with the current position. When something is broken, why fix it?

A simple way to open the conversation with someone who is resistant is to state the problem in clear language and ask for their help in resolving it. This technique is more effective if you pick something small and relevant to the project, but that isn't the goal of the whole project. For example, "The company needs to launch a new product by the end of the quarter because we've promised that to the stock market, so can you help me?" is less effective than, "I'm chairing a meeting next week on possible product ideas but I don't know enough about your area. Can you help me understand?"

There's more about engaging resisters in Chapter 5.

> **The Five Whys exercise**
>
> Five Whys is a creative problem-solving technique and a way of prompting thinking to help identify the root cause of an issue. Ask 'why?' as a response to each answer until you uncover the real cause of the problem.
>
> Here's an example.
>
> Problem: The IT director does not support the project.
>
> Why? Because she thinks what we are doing is too ambitious.
>
> Why? Because she doesn't understand the rationale behind the transformation.
>
> Why? Because she didn't come to the briefing workshops.
>
> Why? Because she wasn't invited.
>
> Why? Because the project team didn't engage her earlier.
>
> Use as many 'whys' as necessary to get to an answer that helps you move forward with problem solving.

2. They are indifferent and you need them to be supportive

People show indifference for several reasons including the fact that they simply don't think your project or problem has any relevance to them. Look for ways to show that it could or should be important to them. If you have a good relationship with them, you could ask them why it appears they are indifferent to your current work when it's important to you (and if you can, name drop some senior stakeholders who might be influential to this person).

Note that you might find out that they are resistant to the project and haven't yet felt willing or able to say as much.

You can use this information to help craft your next steps.

People respond to information in different ways. One stakeholder may need to be presented with statistics and figures to 'get' what the project is all about; another may need to connect with it emotionally, for example through the stories of users or customers. Stories are a powerful way to explain the rationale for a piece of work or decision.

3. They are supportive and you need them to be proactive

You need them to take action and be proactive in their engagement with the project, not just supportive in principle.

Talk to them about why they are supportive of the project. Why do they care about the project?

If they fall into the supportive group, your stakeholder is already showing signs of engagement. The actions you take should build on that engagement, so don't invite them to briefing meetings when they already know the content or otherwise waste their time.

Ask for small commitments that help move the project forward. You can even ask them what they would like to do to support achieving the change you are trying to deliver. Make the most of their support by allowing them to tailor their involvement, as long as it is beneficial for both of you.

Set boundaries on engagement

Would you say yes to a task if you didn't know how long it would take or when it would end? Probably not.

Project stakeholders are the same. They are more likely to give you their time if you tell them how much of it you want, especially time-poor senior leaders in the organisation. Set clear boundaries for the duration and effort required of them to make it easier for people to say yes.

Organisational influences on your project

As well as the influence that people have on how your project unfolds, it's also important to understand other influences from the organisation. The processes and structures in use across the organisation will necessarily shape how you approach the project work, especially communication and engagement activities.

Organisational influences include:

- policies;
- processes;
- procedures;
- internal standards and guidelines;
- infrastructure;
- physical location of offices, resources, facilities and customer-base;
- tools and technology in use for carrying out various tasks e.g. channels for communication;
- lessons learned from previous projects;
- project prioritisation criteria (because knowing where your project is in the hierarchy of prioritisation will help you understand the priority stakeholders will attach to it).

Organisational influences are basically part of the 'the way we work around here'. They create the formal structure for operations. The project is unlikely to be able to influence these things and must run within their constraints.

Planning in complex environments

Planning and scheduling in traditional predictive environments revolve around eliciting the requirements, breaking down the work, sequencing the activities, allocating resources to tasks and then delivering the plan.

In complex environments, that is rarely possible. You probably won't have all the information to build out a schedule right to the end of the project. There are multiple options for sequencing tasks, and resources might not yet be available.

All resources are not created equal, either. Skill levels in the team could be weak, or at best, variable. As the project leader, you may have to exert your influence to get them trained up. That can take time and require a cash investment too, all of which delays the individual making a full contribution to their tasks.

They may not work as efficiently as fully-skilled team members, so their work takes longer, which affects the dates on the schedule.

It's important to consider the people available to do the work as a crucial constraint, even on relatively straightforward projects.

The size of the project often influences complexity but even so-called small projects can be socially and politically complex. It's hard to plan for a linear project life cycle when you can't predict what's going to be happening in even a few months.

Even if the end goal is clear, the route to get there might not be. It can be difficult to schedule human resources when the task they are doing is knowledge work. For example, it could take a subject matter expert three weeks to complete a task, because of the thinking time involved, or their other priorities, when in fact the main part of the task effort was only a few hours. Or it might be hard to predict when a task is going to complete because it relies on external validation or input, with no way of knowing how long an external body might take to turn the work around.

In situations like this, stop thinking that your project will follow the clear-cut paths you are used to. A complex environment demands a different mindset. In *Thriving at the Edge of Chaos*, Jonathan Sapir writes:

> *Adopting a different frame of reference changes one's perspective so that what was remote and unnatural becomes sensible and natural. If the world you work in is complex, then acting congruently with that complexity can be simpler than trying to control it like a machine that doesn't exist.*

In other words, accept that your complex project is going to follow a different path and allow for that in your thinking and actions. Relax into the ambiguity, control what can be controlled and manage what can be managed. Create an environment where people can do their best work. Influence the context to enable the right outcome to emerge.

If you can't accurately anticipate what needs to happen and when it will happen, you can still plan your project to provide some structure to the team.

One tactic to consider is progressive elaboration via rolling wave planning. Progressive elaboration means adding more detail to the plan as the work unfolds. You start by planning the detail of the near-term activities; things you can adequately foresee in the near future. The rest of the plan is drawn with a broad brush: you might only have high level milestones, phases, or in the case of a programme, names of projects to be delivered later.

Planning for GDPR compliance was a challenge. While the end goal was clear (to be compliant with General Data Protection Regulation requirements), for one project team, how to get there was not. When the project team started their prep work, the UK regulator had not released all the information to identify the tasks required. It wasn't clear what, if any, overlap there would be with other incoming legislation, which also hadn't been fully communicated.

The project team didn't want to pause work until the situation was known, as it was clear they would never get through the internal tasks required if they waited. The project was split into workstreams focusing on different areas. Each workstream prioritised achieving compliance with what was known in their area, taking an iterative approach to introducing new requirements and tasks as more information was uncovered. All workstreams worked collaboratively to share knowledge and resources. Solutions were co-created with a common goal.

Communication with stakeholder groups was also done on an iterative basis. Internally, a project newsletter was shared monthly. Each business unit nominated a key individual to be the main point of contact for regular training and updates.

A publicly-facing web page targeted at a particular client group was set up to share the latest information and documentation, along with a guide to what GDPR meant for that client group.

This approach did result in some re-work where documentation had been drafted and needed to be redrafted when new requirements were known. This meant communicating out to clients to let them know the latest information and to make sure they had the updated version of their GDPR guide.

The project manager would not normally have shared information with clients before the full facts were known and a formal, final version of a definitive position could be released. However, the run-up to GDPR coming into force was a socially and politically complex time, with lots of nervousness in the client group about what it meant for them. Although clients ended up with evolving documentation, feedback was incredibly positive. They appreciated being kept informed, even when the situation was not totally understood, because they could see that the project team were actively working to reduce complexity for them.

As the project progresses, the plan is updated. You add in deliverables and schedule tasks for the next period. The time period planned in detail could be any length of time, but 90 days is a good benchmark. That gives you a three-month window to focus on. Each month, update the plan to include work that falls into the next month, so your schedule constantly comprises a detailed view of the next 90 days.

Rolling wave planning is useful because it means work can start on what is known, while planning continues on what is not yet clear. It works best where there is a defined end goal as that helps counteract claims of scope creep.

Rolling wave planning requires a mindset change to work. It's very different from the predictive way of planning a whole project and creating a full schedule at the start. When you've got used to working with a rolling plan, you'll find it is very freeing and allows for a lot of collaboration with stakeholders. You can invest time in resolving uncertainty associated with the sociopolitical complexity of the project, while keeping the pace and showing evidence of delivery.

Rolling wave planning is a technique not limited to predictive project environments. In teams using sprints, sprint planning takes place at the start of a new sprint. The goal for the sprint is set. Prioritised product backlog items that are ready to be worked on are reviewed. The team decides which of these would contribute to the sprint goal and can be completed during the sprint. Then the team decides how to plan the tasks within the sprint. Activities happening in the next couple of sprints are likely to be far better understood and defined than those tabled to be worked on later in the project. Progressive elaboration also allows more detail to be added to user stories and backlog items as the team gets closer to working on them.

Action steps

- Learn more about your preferences for connecting with others by taking the iMA questionnaire for project professionals here: http://ima-pm.co.uk.
- Create a social network diagram for your project, programme or portfolio.
- Look at the strength of your personal network within your organisation. What steps can you take to build relationships with people, even if they aren't currently active stakeholders in your work? Who in your network could you engage with this week to re-energise your relationship? Send them a quick message with something they might find interesting just to keep the connection between you.

- Identify what kind of project structure you have: is it functional, projectised or a matrix?
- Complete an analysis of stakeholder engagement levels for your core stakeholders (or stakeholder groups). What does this tell you about how you should spend your time and energy on communication and engagement activities?

Key takeaways

- A social system is the network of relationships and how they interact and influence each other as a whole.
- A positive project culture counteracts some of the conflict and challenge you can expect in a complex project environment.
- Sociopolitical complexity often relates to people and behaviours. Emotional intelligence and a solid understanding of the human and organisational influences on your project, will help you navigate the complexity more easily.
- The more you understand about the politics, personalities and relationships affecting your project, the greater the chance of being able to operate successfully within that framework.
- Stakeholder engagement can be influenced and can change over time. Someone who is proactively engaged right now might not be in a few months, and vice versa.

3

Engaging and how to do it

Engagement helps drive action on projects. As it is people who do the work, engagement is therefore a contributing factor to getting tasks done on time, to the required scope and at a level of quality that results in stakeholder satisfaction.

This chapter looks at what engagement means in a project environment. It discusses the two elements of projects where engagement is required and covers core techniques for engaging others.

Engagement basics

Let's recap the definition of stakeholder engagement:

> *The systematic identification, analysis, planning and implementation of actions designed to influence stakeholders.*

Essentially, it's all about working with people to build support to achieve the intended outcomes.

The core aspects of engagement are:

- understanding stakeholder perspectives;
- building trusted relationships; and
- taking action and influencing stakeholder perspectives to shape the work in the direction of the intended outcomes.

If those aspects were to be put into a formula, it would look like this:

UNDERSTANDING + ACTION + INFLUENCE = ENGAGEMENT

Understanding stakeholder perspectives

Your stakeholder identification work will have given you a high-level understanding of how an individual stakeholder will interact with and contribute to the project.

Next, it's time to move into the early engagement stage of the stakeholder life cycle.

What issues are they dealing with? How do these affect the project? What point of view do they have about various different aspects of the project? Humans are nuanced. Don't assume that they hold one view about the work. They might be supportive of some aspects but critical of what the change might mean in other areas.

Try to uncover the values that shape their commitment to work. Hopefully you'll find you have values in common; if you work in the same organisation, it's likely that the corporate values are the ones people subscribe to.

Put yourself in their shoes. To be successful at engagement, two things must be understood:

- How stakeholders feel about the project and the effect it will have on them. This is emotional appeal (which you can think of – to use corporate buzzwords – as "winning hearts").
- How confident stakeholders feel that the work being done is the right work. This is rational appeal (which equates to "winning minds").

Table 3.1 shows a summary of what that sounds like from the point of view of a stakeholder. You may never hear these words, but you might hear something like them, or be able to tell from their actions and body language that that is how they are feeling.

	Emotional appeal	Rational appeal
Stakeholder opinion	You have listened to my views	I understand what the project is delivering, even if I don't agree with it
	I believe you've understood my views	I'm confident that the vision is achievable and the schedule is realistic
	I understand what the impact of the project will be on me, my team, my role and my place in the organisation	I'm confident the project team have the skills required to deliver the work
	I believe I've been told the truth	I believe I've been told the truth

Table 3.1 Appealing to emotional and rational aspects of engagement

Stakeholder satisfaction was identified as the most critical success factor in complex projects through a literature review of 27 publications by researchers Rezvani and Khosravi. Their work also identified that poor communication and relationships with stakeholders is joint top (along with poor planning and changing project requirements) of the list of factors that contribute to the failure of complex projects.

The more stakeholder positions can be understood, the more likely it is that you'll be able to deliver something they value and build a successful working relationship with them.

Building trusted relationships

The first actions you need to take are to create relationships with the stakeholders identified.

You can't influence without having a stake in the relationship, so building credible, trusted relationships with stakeholders should be high on your agenda.

Ideally, you will have started building relationships with core stakeholders long before you need to engage them on a project. It is easier to onboard a new stakeholder to your project if you already know something about them and they already know about you. That's why it is valuable to have a strong personal network within your organisation and your wider industry.

Demonstrating that you hold the same values as someone else is a way to build trusting relationships. You do this through your actions and what you say, so make sure the two are congruent. One of the fastest ways to lose trust is to say one thing and do another. People won't know which 'you' to believe, or who will show up on any given day.

It takes work to build relationships. Even if you have an established relationship with a stakeholder, it takes time and commitment to keep that relationship going. We'll look at activities you can do to engage later in this chapter.

Types of influence

There are two types of influence: soft and hard. You exert soft influence when you share knowledge, communicate, engage, inspire and work with others. Hard influence happens in situations where there is no choice: where rules, the law or regulation influence decision making because that's how it has to be. It's easier to get a decision if you can call on hard influence, but there could be plenty of grumbling about it.

How do you create relationships quickly?

It's one thing to say 'build trusted relationships with stakeholders so that you can engage and influence them more effectively' and another to have a project sponsor telling you to get on with the work today. While confident relationships are built over time, there will be some situations where you need to start working with someone quickly. Here are some quick tips for starting your relationship on the right footing for building a professional relationship longer term.

Do what you say you are going to do. If you promise to complete a task or get back to them by a certain time, do it. Be reliable.

Respect their time. Don't make interactions longer than they have to be. Keep emails and other written communication as short as possible.

Help them take the next step. Be explicit about what decision needs to be taken or what you need from them. Stakeholders have other jobs. Don't expect them to instantly know what you need. Make it easy for them to complete their work.

Take notes to help you remember the small things. Next time you speak to them, small talk will be easier as you can ask after their children, or make a comment about their pets, favourite hobby, sports team, TV show or whatever. If they mention something, note it down to use in a future conversation.

Ask what you can do for them. "Is there anything else I should be doing for you?" or "How else can I help you?" shows you are interested and willing to listen. (People will be grateful you asked, and most of the time, the answer will be no.)

Say thank you. A bit of gratitude goes a long way.

It's important to understand how soft and hard influence can work together. Hard influence might force through a project change, but without soft influence running alongside it, the required action or behaviour doesn't happen after all. In a project delivery role, you are most likely to be using soft influence to affect change, but hard influence may also come into play, for example, when the CEO decides a particular course of action is the way forward. When that happens, remember to link soft influence actions in with how you move forward to get the best result for your stakeholders and project.

Engaging and how to do it

Influencing stakeholder perspectives

If someone is influencing you, you don't switch from being against their point of view to suddenly 100 per cent supportive. Being influenced happens on a sliding scale.

Back in 1958, Herbert Kelman researched the extent to which influence happens. He concluded that changes in attitudes and actions as a result of being influenced occur at different levels. In other words, even if three people are influenced to behave the same way, they could accept the influence in different ways.

He identified three different processes of influence:

1. **Compliance**: The individual doesn't believe in the behaviour they demonstrate, but they do as they are told anyway.
   Example: Someone following a health and safety policy to wear protective clothing when they feel it is overkill for the small job they are doing.
2. **Identification**: The individual changes their behaviour to align with the request or behaviour of another individual or group. The act of conforming is more important than what they are conforming with.
   Example: Someone whose attitude to a project changes when they see how important it is to the CEO.
3. **Internalisation**: The individual fully believes in the behaviour or position they have been influenced to adopt because it aligns with their personal value system.
   Example: Someone who reduces their use of single-use plastic at home after working on a corporate social responsibility project to achieve the same aim at the office.

When you understand the different ways people can be influenced, you can be more conscious about the action you take.

Before you can influence anyone, you need to work out what you are trying to get them to do. Once you have a clear objective, you can then start influencing.

There are typically three ways that you can influence:

- influencing up: working with your manager or sponsor;
- influencing across: working with your peers and team; and
- influencing out: working with other people beyond the immediate team.

In all of these cases, you can influence *through* others as well as influence an individual directly. For example, let's say the team has recently been unhappy about the perceived requirement to work late. You don't know exactly how it has happened, but the team seem to be staying later in the evening, not at your request. You've made it clear you are happy for people to leave the office on time, but it isn't happening.

You chat to a couple of senior members of the team to find out more about what's happened, and it appears to be a peer pressure situation. One of the team has a bit too much work and that's started a slide towards presenteeism in the other team members. You address the workload problem for the individual. You ask a senior member of the team to make an effort to leave on time. Their behaviour influences the other team members, and the presenteeism problem is resolved.

Influencing is an active state: you have to do or say something to influence another person. Project professionals are often wary of being seen as influential. Influencing others can feel slightly manipulative or dishonest, especially if you have been taught to remain neutral and facilitate the project process.

It's time to put those feelings aside. Influencing isn't something to avoid. You do it all the time, whether it's saying, "I fancy a takeaway for dinner," or talking about the great location for a holiday you've seen online. Turning up late to a meeting influences others into believing that is appropriate behaviour. You influence and shape other people's behaviour every day, even if you aren't aware of it.

Very few project professionals turn up to work and write 'influencing' as a task on their To Do list for the day. Often, the act of influencing happens while going about other daily tasks. It is wrapped into other types of professional behaviour and interactions with colleagues.

However, the more you understand about how your behaviour and actions influences others, the more conscious you can be of how what you do can effect change and lead to better project outcomes.

Successful stakeholder relationships rely on you being conscious of the influencing you are doing, thinking through the impact of that and making appropriate decisions about the actions you take.

What are you engaging them in?

You know 'engagement' is important on projects, but that begs the question: what exactly are you engaging them in?

There are two things that you should be engaging your project stakeholders in: the project deliverables and the process.

Project deliverables

First, stakeholders should be engaged in the purpose of the project. You are delivering something (outputs) and it has some benefit for the organisation (outcomes).

Stakeholders should understand why the project is happening, what the overall vision is, why it's good for the organisation and what the benefits are.

This can be an easy message if the benefits are clear and something the stakeholder wants. However, it's a different story if the benefits are less clear and/or the stakeholder never wanted them in the first place.

Project management process

Second, stakeholders should be engaged in the project management process. Some of the people you work with will not have had much experience working on projects, or the team might be new to working together, even if individuals have worked on projects.

Part of your engagement activity should be explaining what is happening on the project. This includes making sure everyone understands their roles and responsibilities, their tasks, the process for making decisions, what a risk is and what to do if they think of one and anything else that helps the team work together efficiently.

Many project sponsors are not experienced in the role and have not had any training on what it means to be an effective sponsor. You may also have to engage them in the process of sponsorship, by explaining and encouraging them so that they feel confident to carry out the sponsor's duties.

When to do engagement

Stakeholder engagement is something to do throughout the project life cycle. The activities you do will depend on where you are in the project life cycle and where the stakeholder is in their life cycle with the project, but engagement starts at the moment you're considering whether someone is a stakeholder on your project and ends after they walk away from the project.

However, engagement doesn't always happen to the timetable you've carefully mapped out. For example, maybe you have to delay a discussion with key stakeholders because someone is off sick, because the risk of going ahead means missing something.

Ideally, the initial engagement comes before creating a project schedule. Then you can use what you learn in those early discussions to shape your project timeline.

I was working on a software implementation project where we needed to install the same solution in multiple hospitals. We selected the order to complete the installations, based on which locations were close to each other, what other projects those sites were involved with and engagement levels of the management and clinical teams at each place (picking those assessed as 'most supportive' first, followed by the most challenging to make sure they would be finished by the end date, then other locations towards the end).

Our project involved installing new shelving, desks, wiring, electrical sockets and network points in clinical areas that previously hadn't had any IT equipment.

During the kick off meeting at one location, we talked about the refurbishment work we would be carrying out on site. The office manager explained they had their own refurb plans. A few weeks after we were due to finish, they were moving some hospital departments around to make better use of the space.

As we talked, we realised they would be ripping out everything we had just installed to make space for other equipment. Their plans included relocating the clinical area we were refurbishing.

It didn't make business sense to do that. As no work had taken place and no orders for equipment had been made, it was easy to switch the timing of that hospital with another. We worked on another implementation and came back to their hospital later in the year, when their reorganisation work was complete.

The project team continued to engage with that hospital's management team throughout their local development. Because of that, they were able to make some provision for wires and cables as they carried out their work. That saved time and disruption when we came back to complete the software installation later that year.

Table 3.2 shows examples of activities for the project manager to take with regard to engaging stakeholders at different points in a project.

Project step[3]	Example activities for project manager
Definition	Agree working relationships with the whole team Debate and agree scope/requirements/user stories Ensure stakeholders have an aligned view of scope Make it possible for stakeholders to talk to one another
Design and plan	Consult on solution design Negotiate for resources Gain sign off for design Agree success criteria Engage stakeholder in estimating effort/duration of work Co-create plan/schedule for next steps and gain commitment to delivery Capture and implement lessons learned
Build/Implement	Hold regular discussions/meetings with stakeholder to inform them of progress and gain updates on their work Consult regarding change requests Capture and implement feedback on processes used for lessons learned Escalate issues as appropriate Secure support for test priorities and provide feedback on testing activities Facilitate the resolution of conflict Ongoing management of expectations
Handover	Deliver training Facilitate handover Continue to capture, implement and share lessons learned Thank stakeholder for their participation and support

Table 3.2 Example stakeholder engagement activities based on project step

[3] Note that this is not meant to be representative of any one project life cycle, method or approach. Whether you work with predictive, iterative or hybrid methods, you should be able to identify steps on your project journey and align them to typical activities to be undertaken at that time with project stakeholders.

Table 3.3 shows examples of activities for the project manager to take in relation to where the stakeholder is in their life cycle of engagement with the project.

You'll see lessons learned in various places in both those tables. It's so important to continually collect and act on feedback from stakeholders as you go through the project. On one project, we were able to improve stakeholder satisfaction scores from four out of 10 to nine out of 10 by listening and acting on continuous feedback. The case study that explains how I achieved this (with my team) is explained in another of my books, *Customer-Centric Project Management* so

Stakeholder life cycle phase	Example activities for project manager
Identification	Deliver initial briefing about the project Hold one-to-one discussions about goals, objectives, stakeholder expectations Define roles and responsibilities Introduce stakeholder to core project team
Early engagement	Agree project scope Agree project tasks stakeholder is responsible for Invite stakeholder to team meetings Add stakeholder to mailing lists for reporting Consult with stakeholder on solution/next steps Provide support and documentation to ensure they feel comfortable to contribute
Mature engagement	Hold ongoing individual discussions and discussions as part of a group to ensure progress is being made Ensure stakeholder participates appropriately in team meetings Consult with and keep in touch as required Gather lessons learned from the stakeholder
Dissolution	Ensure all stakeholder's activities are complete Ensure stakeholder is satisfied with the outcome of their contribution Gather lessons learned from the stakeholder Thank the stakeholder

Table 3.3 Examples of engagement activities based on stakeholder life cycle

here all I want to say is that engagement very much benefits from responding to feedback and you don't have to wait until the end of the project to get any.

Ultimately, the bottom line to remember is do as much stakeholder engagement as you can, all the time. Pretty much every project management activity that involves someone else can be seen as stakeholder engagement. Just make sure you are engaging them and not boring them or encouraging them to be disinterested!

Working in a network

You might be a single person, with relationships that stretch out to many other individuals, but your organisation does not operate on a point-to-point basis, as Figure 3.1 shows – and even that is highly stylised and simplified. Try to recreate this diagram for a team you work in. You might need a large piece of paper!

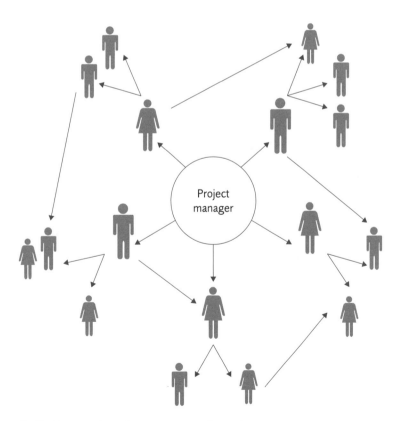

Figure 3.1 Connections between people and teams

Stakeholders talk to each other. They respect each other (or not). There is politics in any organisation. If you don't see it, that could be because it's so aligned to how you work that it's transparent to you. However, the informal power structures that shape how decisions are taken and what gets done are there, whether they are obvious to you or not.

Understanding the alliances and how different stakeholders or groups interact in the organisation will help you decide what actions to take to be the most influential.

Engaging across multiple projects

Often, stakeholders work on several different projects at the same time, especially knowledge workers and those with specific subject matter expertise.

Coordinate your engagement and influencing activity across the projects, programmes and portfolios where individuals are involved. There's nothing more annoying than having five project managers each ask you for virtually the same information about your department. Why couldn't they talk to each other and use the information you sent to the first person?

> Good communication between project delivery teams can minimise the amount of annoyance for stakeholders. On a software project, I needed to know the number of medical secretaries employed by hospitals or self-employed but based across several business units to estimate licence costs. I knew that a data protection project had collected this information a few months earlier. Working with that project manager, I was able to get adequate information for the estimate without having to ask business unit managers for information they had provided to someone else, just a few months before.
>
> Minimising the annoyance factor means your communications are more likely to be read and acted on when you need them to because people don't feel that they are wasting their time.

Make sure stakeholder engagement activities are properly communicated within the programme and portfolio teams. A stakeholder may only have influence over one project, but that influence could have a programme-wide impact. Programme managers can actively ensure that stakeholders are engaged intelligently across the projects they are involved in.

The challenge of time

I ran a survey of my blog readers, asking what prevented them from doing stakeholder engagement the way they wanted to. Over 30 per cent of them responded saying they didn't have time.[4]

Project, programme and portfolio management is often a high stress, busy job. But stakeholder engagement is such a valuable activity that it can't be pushed to the bottom of the To Do list. From a delivery perspective, the end users don't care if you had a tidy risk log during the project. They care that they knew what was going on, they had a chance to air their views and they got the deliverables they wanted from the project.

Look at how you are spending your time and consider whether it is adequately balanced. The vast majority of your time should be spent on engaging with others to get the work done.

Techniques for engagement

Engagement can be formal and overt, such as sending out a briefing message or having a meeting with a stakeholder. It can also be informal, like a quick chat or a check in by text message. It can also be subtle and more covert, for example, including a sceptical stakeholder in a site visit to a crumbling building to show them why a renovation project is needed.

Any time you are talking to or working with another person, you have the opportunity to engage them. Share your enthusiasm, encourage their contribution. Be nice to be around. The alternative extreme is broadcasting at them, taking a command-and-control approach or not treating them as a human being with agency. You wouldn't want to be on the receiving end of that, so why impose it on your colleagues?

Not only will taking an 'engagement first' approach get you better results for your project, you'll also be acting like a professional; someone who is easy to work with.

Of course, there will be moments where you won't feel like being enthusiastic about your work, or you have to have a difficult conversation and say no to someone. That's part of the job and also part of having boundaries around your role and the project's scope. You can still engage with people at these times, by

[4] https://www.girlsguidetopm.com/why-dont-50-of-people-do-stakeholder-engagement/

explaining the rationale, asking for their support with the decision and following up if they have further questions.

Below, you'll find an inexhaustive list of techniques for engaging others on projects.

Expectation mapping

What it is: A way of recording what people are expecting to get or expecting to happen as a result of the project.

Good for: Understanding where there might be areas of conflict or misunderstanding.

How to do it: Create a table that records the stakeholder name and their expectations, or include an 'expectations' column in your stakeholder register. Ask each individual or group representative what they think the project is going to do for them/the business to establish what they are expecting from it unless you already have a very clear idea of what they are going to say.

When you have completed the list of expectations, compare and contrast what people think they are going to be getting. Look for conflicts in expectations, e.g. where one stakeholder group thinks something will be delivered and the sponsor does not believe that will be the case.

Take action on any misaligned expectations by going back to the requirements documentation, checking scope elements and making sure people have a common understanding of what the project will deliver.

Concerns mapping

What it is: Similar to expectations mapping, concerns mapping is a way of recording what people are worried about on a project.

Good for: Understanding where there might be areas of conflict and uncovering risk.

How to do it: Create a table that records the stakeholder name and the things they are worried about in relation to the project process or deliverables, or include a 'concerns' column in your stakeholder register. Talk to each stakeholder or group representative to find out what concerns they have. People may be reluctant to share concerns so openly at the beginning of a project, so you can return to this table throughout the project and update it.

Use the data in the table to compare and contrast the worries people have shared. Some might be easy to address. Others might require further discussion.

Transfer anything relevant to the risk or issue logs where you can actively manage them.

Make a note to follow up with stakeholders who expressed concerns, so they know you listened and are taking steps where you can. Even if you can't do anything about a concern, let the person who raised it know that you have taken their perspective on board.

Personal contacts notebook

What it is: An easy way of remembering details to build rapport with stakeholders and team members.

Good for: People who struggle to remember names or make small talk!

How to do it: Get an A-Z indexed notebook. Write the names of stakeholders in your notebook, ordered by first name to make it easier to find their details afterwards (unless you are a whizz at remembering people's surnames). Add their job title, role on the project and contact info.

Leave a few blank lines between each stakeholder on each page so you've got space to add more information about them.

Why paper? I prefer the security of knowing that my notes are locked away in my home office. However, if you prefer digital note-keeping, by all means create a digital stakeholder record in a secure system.

As you find out information about the individuals through the course of your normal conversations, record that in your notes. The next time you meet the person, quickly look back over your notes to remind yourself of anything you can drop into conversation.

Don't make your conversation sound forced. For example, let's say one day they tell you the name of their child. In a conversation a few weeks later, they mention they are taking their son to football lessons. You can drop their son's name, because you have a system for remembering it. It sounds natural and shows you were listening last time.

If you are going to keep personal data about individuals, make sure you do so in alignment with relevant data protection protocols and regulations. Update your entries regularly as people change jobs or move locations within the business.

Tip: Don't add notebook entries for every single person you meet in the course of your work. It's far more valuable to focus on the internal colleagues and key suppliers you will have a relationship with over time, especially senior managers who may crop up as a project stakeholder again in the future.

The more you can personalise your engagement, the more successful it will be. In *Yes! 50 Secrets from the Science of Persuasion*, the authors share research by Randy Garner that shows a personal message goes a long way.

Garner sent out paper surveys with a request for recipients to fill them in. Recipients either got:

- a handwritten sticky note asking them to complete the survey, stuck on to the cover letter;
- a handwritten note written directly on to the cover letter; or
- no handwritten note (just the survey and cover letter).

More than 75 per cent of people who received the version with the sticky note went on to fill out the survey. Just under 50 per cent of those who got the handwritten note on the letter filled in their surveys. And only 36 per cent of people who received no handwritten note bothered to complete theirs.

Garner concluded that people recognise the effort you've gone to in writing a personalised note and are more likely to respond. In fact, the survey respondents with the sticky notes provided more detailed answers and returned their surveys more quickly.

When you are planning your engagement efforts, whether that's inviting users to a focus group or sending out reports, think about how you can personalise the interaction to increase the likelihood of a positive response.

Using others to engage

What it is: Identifying influential individuals who could help shape the direction of your project and engaging with them, with the aim of using their influence to engage more widely.

Good for: Reaching communities you cannot reach alone; amplifying your message.

How to do it: First, you need to be clear on the outcome that you want to achieve. Consider who can help you achieve that. Look for people with formal and informal power within the organisation, with links to the communities you want to reach.

Engage them in the project if they are not already involved. Find a role for them where they can be valuable and feel like they are making a useful contribution. You can be straight up and ask them for help in engaging the communities you are struggling to reach, or you can assume that they'll network and informally do what you are hoping, to raise awareness or create some positivity for your project.

Celebrating success

What it is: An opportunity to say thank you to someone, or a team, for their contribution.

Good for: Building morale, re-engaging team members, creating a PR opportunity to talk about your project (i.e. you had a success worth celebrating. Staff magazines and internal comms teams are often on the lookout for good news stories to share).

How to do it: There are a myriad of ways of celebrating success. Choose something that is accessible for all team members. After work drinks at the pub will not suit those in the team who do not drink or who have childcare responsibilities and need to get home. Ideally, celebrate in working hours.

Here are some suggestions.

Food: If the team is small, go out for something to eat, or have a pot luck in the office or a picnic (take a frisbee or outdoor games). Bring cakes to a project meeting. Send chocolates in the post to virtual team members. Order pizza to go to everyone's house at the same time.

Games: Take time out of the working day to play ping pong, table football, go bowling or similar.

Say 'Thank you': It costs nothing to say thank you and it's my belief that you should do so as often as possible. You can never appreciate people too much. And you don't have to wait for a significant milestone to do so. Just say it whenever. You can also email a thank you message. Some people will appreciate this more as they can file it away for their end of year review more easily than if you had simply said it in passing. It seems to count even more if you can get a senior manager to send the message.

Staff scheme: Many employers have staff recognition schemes that can be used to thank colleagues for a job well done. In my last role, the corporate recognition scheme mainly offered thank you messages which were shared on an internal website, but there was also an option for senior managers to gift shopping vouchers.

Small gifts: Your project budget or department budget might stretch to small gifts like vouchers for the local coffee shop.

> **Other celebration ideas**
> At the close of one multi-year project, I bought each team member a bottle of wine from the year that they started on the project.
> Our project team went to a comedy club. Some of the acts fell flat, but others were fantastic. We created a shared experience too so it doubled as a team-building event.

If you don't instinctively know what your team would like from this list, or you can't tell if they would like any of them, then you don't know your team very well. That's OK, it happens. Especially on big teams.

The best way to find out how people would like to be thanked is to ask them. Yes, it takes away some of the spontaneity but generally people would much rather get something they want than something they don't value. Most individuals will appreciate the fact that you care enough to thank them in a way that is meaningful to them.

You can celebrate project milestones, completed project phases, successful delivery (of anything) but also personal moments in the team such as birthdays and anniversaries of people joining the team or the company. Don't forget national holidays. These double up as a good way to learn more about the culture and countries of people in your international team.

Active project marketing

What it is: Marketing can be thought of as a planned series of tasks with the objective of promoting your project to a wide audience.

Good for: Getting your message out far and wide, which contributes to building interest in your project and raising the awareness of what you are doing. If people feel that the project is a worthwhile undertaking and that other people care about the project (by giving it space in your internal newsletter etc.) then they are more likely to comply with your requests for cooperation.

How to do it: Identify the main messages you want to get across about the project. Think about who should be the spokesperson to share those messages. Plan how best to communicate the messages e.g. presentations, roadshows, internal communications tools, newsletters, promotions or competitions etc. Consider the budget and time commitments of each option and build what you want to do into your communications plan.

Using social proof

Social proof is a marketing concept that says you are more likely to take action if you see that other people already have. It's why we check reviews on websites before we buy something.

You can use the same approach on your projects. People are more likely to get involved if they can see that others are already involved and haven't been negatively affected. Find some customer stories, share successes, talk about what the project has achieved and how much fun it is working together. Take photos of your team out and about. Think of every opportunity as a moment to get some good internal publicity.

Actively seek input

Engagement is more than holding meetings, emailing out status reports and putting an article up on the intranet. Look for ways that you can actively seek input from the people who matter.

Examples include:

- Change your email signature to include a link to a project email inbox or 'contact us' form.
- If you write an article for the company magazine, include a phone number, email address or equivalent so people can get in touch.
- Include contact information on your last slide of a presentation, or in the footer of each slide or page in your document.
- Send out a survey.
- Drop in to working sessions like system testing and find out how things are going, getting feedback from people doing the work.
- Let people know that you are available and interested in their thoughts. Ask for input and questions at meetings: don't let meetings turn into a broadcast session for you and your ideas.

Once I put a sticker on my name tag at an internal company conference that said 'Ask me about [name of project].' I wanted to let people know what I was working on and invite questions. Plus, it was a useful icebreaker with people in the queue for coffee.

Informal opportunities

What it is: Simply being ready to talk about your project to any interested person, at any time.

Good for: Moments where you bump into key stakeholders and want to use the opportunity to discuss your project.

How to do it: Just be ready! Carry around your action log or a one-pager on what your project is all about to use as a conversation prompt or an opportunity to remind people what actions they should be focused on. Or create opportunities, for example:

- Make sure you are in the lift with someone you need to speak to.
- Catch someone you have been trying to speak to at the end of the day and walk them out to their car (if you can do so without coming across as annoying).
- Call someone with information they will find useful and while on the phone ask them for an update on their project tasks.

Three examples of making the most of informal opportunities

1. I worked in Paris for a few years, in a central function that supported internal communications teams around the world. We had a number of products, web tools and projects that we managed. We were a very niche team and not many people understood the international processes we supported. My boss at the time had a one-page slide that he carried around, tucked in the back of his folder. It was a visual representation of the role of the department and our core initiatives that made it clear what we did. He used it regularly, whipping it out in conversations to explain the role of the team. Sometimes a visual prompt like a slide is better than having an elevator pitch message, although it is a good idea to have both.

2. In another role, I found myself evacuating the building on a fire drill and walking down the stairs next to the CEO. He asked me my opinion about a project and I was able to give him an honest answer because I had the information to hand. I would never have normally got an audience with the CEO to discuss this particular software product, but I was able to influence how he felt about whether to invest in the upgrade because I could share the facts I knew.

3. Peter Taylor shared a story with me about a project manager who just couldn't get any time or attention from a key stakeholder. She learned that he had a weekly pizza meeting with his team every Tuesday after work and so she 'hijacked the pizza guy' and stuck a message to the top of the first pizza box that said her name and that she needed five minutes with the stakeholder. She waited outside the room and shortly the stakeholder emerged smiling, congratulated her on her creativity and agreed to meet her the next day.

Communication

Some of the techniques above may be familiar from your work on preparing a communications plan. A large element of engagement is communicating with the right people at the right time, in the right level of detail and with a specific goal in mind to help them take action.

Engagement involves active participation on the part of the person being engaged, so distributing comms materials alone is not engagement – although it's a valid project activity in the right circumstances.

Much communication that needs to be shared on projects can be defined as technical writing because it meets one or more of the following characteristics as defined by the Society for Technical Communications[5].

- It communicates about technical or specialist topics: projects typically deliver in a specialist field or industry.
- It is communicated by using technology: projects rely on intranets, the web and collaboration and communication tools to share messages.
- It provides instructions about how to do something: projects frequently need to provide user instructions, even if those instructions do not relate to the use of technology e.g. business process instructions or requests for information that need the response to be formatted in a certain way.

In her book, *Technical Writing for Business People*, Carrie Marshall lays out seven steps for creating and publishing technical communications, which provide a useful framework for project communications too. They are:

---

[5] See https://www.stc.org/about-stc/defining-technical-communication/

Engaging stakeholders on projects

1. Identifying the specification, audience and scope.
2. Planning.
3. Research and writing.
4. Testing, reviewing and revising.
5. Delivering the communication.
6. Evaluating and collating feedback.
7. Revising (again), archiving and destruction at end of life.

This full process highlights the requirement to build in a feedback loop and engage with recipients to revise and improve even after the message has been shared with one group.

Before undertaking any project communications, there are three core questions to answer:

1. Who are you communicating with?
2. What are you communicating about?
3. How are you going to communicate?

Who are you communicating with?

Use your stakeholder analysis to identify who is going to receive the communication. Put stakeholders into groups related to the type and frequency of communication you intend to do.

For example, your core project team will attend the daily standup, or get meeting notes from weekly project team meetings. Stakeholders you classify as being in the 'early engagement' or 'mature engagement' part of their life cycle could get a weekly roundup report of project progress. External stakeholders will get communication messages when there is something that pertains specifically to their involvement or that they need to know.

Some stakeholders will require detailed information; others simply need to know the project is happening. Knowing who the message is going to allows you to communicate in an appropriate level of detail.

The general principle here is that you tailor who receives what communication based on what they need to know, when they need to know it and what you expect them to do with it.

What are you communicating about?

Different types of messages need different types of delivery methods, so consider what you are trying to say and what you want the resulting action to be (if any).
Messages can be broken down into three categories:

1. Inspirational: Used to explain the programme's vision and mission and helping people see the end-state when the change is delivered.
2. Informational: General project news and information sharing where little engagement is expected beyond reading and digesting.
3. Actionable: Instructions to be carried out by the individual or group.

There are lots of different messages you'll need to communicate during the project including:

- introducing new people to the team;
- sharing the vision, mission and roadmap of the programme;
- delivering training material;
- providing practical direction and guidance about what the upcoming changes mean for a team or individual; and
- 'transactional' communication relating to completing actions and carrying out project tasks.

Before you communicate, pause for a moment and reflect on what the message actually is. Can you make it shorter? Can you provide an example to help people understand?
Build a feedback loop into what you are communicating as a way to check if the communication has been understood by both parties. For example:

- Ask a follow up question: "Now we've gone over that, what are your next steps going to be?"
- Ask them to reply to you (use voting buttons on email to make this easier) confirming the task is complete.
- Summarise your discussion in writing and ask them to confirm it's an accurate reflection of what you agreed.
- Summarise what you have heard from the stakeholder and ask them to confirm you have understood correctly.

- Provide a quiz or test.
- Ask what resources would be helpful for them to share the same message with their colleagues.

How are you communicating?

There is a wide range of tools at your disposal for communicating on projects. Everything from email to slide decks, webinars to infographics, internal social networks and chat apps.

Before you use technology to communicate, make sure everyone you need to communicate with has access to the tech and is actively using it.

Be creative and use the full range of what is available to you. Sometimes communicating in an unexpected way will be the thing that gets the message across.

Tailor the type of message to a delivery mode that will make it most successful. The best way to communicate will depend on the outcome you're seeking. Drawing on the work of Patrick Mayfield, some sample engagement modes for interactions with more or less certainty in the outcome are shown in Figure 3.2.

For example, where you have less certainty about where the communication will end up, opt for a delivery style with high interactivity, like a conversation. Where you already know the outcome you seek, a less interactive style could work, like a presentation.

Tailor the timing of your message to what you think will get the best outcome. Just-in-time communication works well where you are concerned your message may get lost in all the other information being shared.

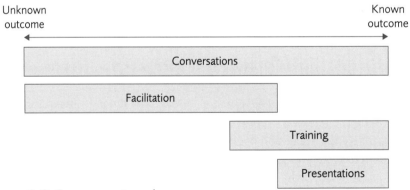

Figure 3.2 Engagement modes

Source: Adapted from Mayfield, 2013

Remember, though, to allow enough space between messages so that people aren't overwhelmed with being on the receiving end of too much communication that is too similar in delivery style.

> **Countdown communication**
> On one project that required multiple business leaders to take multiple actions over several weeks, I sent out 'countdown' emails. Each email's subject line was '4 weeks to go! [Project Name]' and so on. The emails went out at a regular time each week and included the actions to be taken that week.
> This approach helped people stay on top of their actions and make progress each week instead of leaving them all their tasks until the last minute. It also provided a regular reminder point in the week highlighting the criticality of taking those steps.

Stakeholder engagement should definitely be seen as an allied activity to project communications. Make sure your comms plan and your engagement plans work together. If you have different people tasked with managing project communications and leading on core stakeholder relationships, then they should work together to ensure their work is complementary.

There isn't space here to go deeper into project communications, but there are selected resources for further reading in the bibliography.

Engaging project sponsors

The most important relationship for a project manager is that with the project sponsor. The sponsor's support is crucial in achieving the project's aims and objectives.

However, you still need to actively engage with sponsors. Simply having 'sponsor' added to their long list of daily responsibilities is not enough to guarantee that someone will actively participate in the way you need them to for the project to be successful.

Project sponsors often have many demands on their time and several projects they are sponsoring. You want them to be actively engaged with your project, so it is important to build a positive working relationship. Ideally you want them to feel inclined to open and read your emails amongst the hundreds they get every day.

Below are some suggestions for how to make the best of your relationship with the project sponsor.

Flex your style to suit their preferences

Do you make lists or do you doodle mind maps? Do you follow the recipe to cook dinner, or make it up as you go along?

Everyone has different preferences for taking in information and interacting with others. It's your job to learn what works best for your sponsor and tailor your interactions accordingly.

Find out what you can about the sponsor before you meet them for the first time. Talk to people who have worked with them before. Try to uncover their communication preferences and working styles – anything that will help you pitch your communication most effectively.

If you can't find these things out in advance, ask the sponsor for their preferences when you first get a chance to talk to them.

If you don't want to ask them outright how they would like to be communicated with, watch them in meetings. Listen to how they talk. Are they focused on the human stories behind the project? Do they respond well to data and figures? Do they approach problems from a logical or emotional perspective, or somewhere in between?

They may prefer to see a diagram or a prototype over a technical specification document. They may prefer a voicemail over an email. Listen, observe and test your communications with your sponsor. Adapt how you engage with them to get the best results for you both.

Respect their time

Structure how you engage with them to set expectations and show you respect their time. For example, if you say you are going to provide a short status update every Friday, then do so. They may be relying on it for their onward and upward communication.

If you meet with them, even informally, have a few bullet points of what you want to get out of the time so you can both prepare. Start and end your meeting on time. Be prepared to condense the time you thought you had into the 10 minutes they actually have available for you that day: know what on your agenda should take priority.

When the meeting finishes, ask what else they need from you, or what else you can help them with.

When you talk with them, use clear and unambiguous terminology. Avoid the inevitable project jargon that will have sprung up around your project. You and the core team might understand all the acronyms, but the sponsor isn't living and breathing the project like you are.

Senior leaders are sometimes reticent about asking for explanations of things they don't understand, so make it easy for them. Be clear in your communication as that will also help them understand what you require them to do. If you need them to take an action, ask outright for them to do so. They aren't mind-readers and some sponsors won't step in until you ask them to for fear of being accused of micro-managing, or because they aren't close enough to the detail to fully take action without your support.

Show you can be trusted

Sponsors may need to share confidential information with you. They need to know you can handle access to that confidential information in an appropriate way. They need to be able to trust you. Honour their confidences and respect the position they have in the organisation.

Trust takes time to build, so don't expect it to be there overnight. However, it takes seconds to lose the trust of someone, so be conscious of how you are acting with your sponsor. In particular, focus on:

- doing what you said you were going to do and delivering on your promises;
- completing tasks they have asked you to do;
- escalating problems with a couple of recommendations for next steps.

If you can, and you feel it's appropriate to do so, try to get to know your project sponsor as a person. You don't have to be their best friend, but some level of personal connection will also help you build a trusting relationship.

Demonstrate your competence

Meet deadlines. Talk about the progress the team is making before your sponsor asks to hear about it. Add your professional certifications to your email signature. Leave a copy of your professional body magazine on your desk – yes, seriously!

People do notice this stuff and it all helps to paint a picture of you as a competent, safe pair of hands.

Your project sponsor, and stakeholders in general, want to feel secure in the individual they have chosen to lead the project. They want to know that you know what to do.

There is more on building credibility in Chapter 7.

Tell the truth

Your project should have a culture of no surprises. No sponsor likes to be blindsided in a meeting because someone else around the table knows more about their project than they do.

Be honest and be fast in your communication, especially when it comes to sharing potentially bad news.

One of the roles of the project sponsor is to help deal with problems. They can't do that if they don't know about them. Be truthful in your communication and never try to hide an issue. You can always say what you are proactively doing to deal with a problem and let them know you'll update them in 24 hours when you might be asking for their support in resolving it.

Sponsors appreciate being informed. You're giving them information that helps them do their job more effectively. If you think you are sharing too much detail with them, ask what they think. Would they prefer reporting by exception, or are they happy with the level of detail you're providing? Set some parameters around what needs to be mentioned to them and what problems you can handle yourself to save them getting involved. These parameters may change over time as they come to trust your judgement more.

These steps won't guarantee your sponsor is engaged the whole way through your project, but if you can build a good working relationship with them, they are more likely to take your calls and be there when you need them. The suggestions above will also help you spot changes in behaviour so you can identify when a sponsor seems to be taking a step back from engaging with the project. Then you can take action to understand and influence that as necessary.

Engagement in a crisis

Whether it's a supplier going bust or a global pandemic, at some point in your career you're going to have to deal with a crisis.

Here are some tips for staying in control in the moment:

- You need to recognise that there is a crisis before you can act on it, so start creating a regular habit now to reflect on how the project is going. This will make it easier to stop and reflect in times of trouble. Schedule time in the project and your personal calendar to pause and evaluate so reflection becomes part of the cadence of your work.
- Build good relationships with project team members and stakeholders so you can draw on those when times are tough. Build trust ahead of time (although you can't always see a crisis coming) so your communications are credible.
- Communicate transparently and honestly, with sensitivity and inclusivity. Share what you don't yet know as well as what you do.
- If you communicate something that turns out not to be true (or is no longer true) then state that. Don't try to justify or explain – people won't listen to your justification and may not choose to believe it anyway. Simply state that what was previously communicated was not correct or is no longer the case.
- Be respectful of people's time and other commitments. A crisis situation for you might not be a crisis for them – or they may be responding to it differently because of the way it impacts them.
- Make sure you are clear about your own personal values and the ethical boundaries you set for yourself. Make decisions using that value framework and the things you consider non-negotiables. It's harder to cope with criticism and doubt if you are not fully behind your own decisions.
- In a crisis, there are often external influences such as global events over which you can have no control. You may not have all the information you would like to make a decision. Make the decision that feels right for you, and don't dwell on alternative choices or look back with regret. You can't change the past, and you acted in good faith with the information you had at the time.
- Think of one small step you can do to keep moving forward. You don't have to fix everything at once – and you probably can't. Take a small action either to help the project's momentum or to help yourself deal with the situation.
- Practice self-care, whether that's a bath, a glass of wine, a walk with the dog or something else. Like they say before take-off: put your own oxygen mask on before helping others.

Resilience is a key strength for teams and individuals, and is especially important in times of crisis. Nassim Taleb's book, *Antifragile*, discusses the concept that things that are resilient resist shocks and stay the same while things that are antifragile get better and better. Build resilience and antifragility in your team to better deal with problems by creating a learning culture that accepts and embraces mistakes and adapts and grows when faced with problems.

Foster emotional and social intelligence across the team, use empathy and listening skills, and stay curious. Ask questions in a crisis to help understand the issues and how they are affecting the team.

Look out for each other, stand up for each other and recognise that this crisis is only temporary.

The decision to not engage

You don't have to engage with everyone, all the time. There's a truism that communication has to be early and often; that is a general principle, but not a rule. Some situations require you to hold back on sharing information to make sure you have the full picture, or because engaging too early will result in stakeholders forgetting what you told them at the point they need the information.

In some cases, it might be prudent to ignore a stakeholder, or play down their involvement in a project. Good analysis of the situation and the potential impact caused by taking a 'do not engage' approach will help you determine whether this is the best course of action.

The decision not to engage should be an active one. Like any 'do nothing' response to a project situation, it should be considered and evaluated like the other options. If you think it's the best approach, go for it. There's no rule that says you need to engage with all stakeholders.

How to tell if engagement is working

Stakeholder engagement can take lots of different forms. The examples given earlier in this chapter are a non-exclusive list of ways to work with others on projects. You will no doubt have your own ideas and preferences as well.

The engagement formula presents the expectation that you will be influencing stakeholders to do something or behave differently. Engagement in the project is the by-product of understanding the situation and taking action to influence behaviour.

UNDERSTANDING + ACTION + INFLUENCE = ENGAGEMENT

So how do you know if it's working?

It is important to evaluate your engagement activity so you can see if your actions are having the desired effect. If they aren't, you can make changes and do something else. If they are, you'll know to continue with the actions you are currently doing – at least, for now.

Engagement is something you should keep under constant review. What works today may not work as effectively, if at all, in the future.

How to evaluate engagement

Every engagement activity should have a specific goal, for example:

- to communicate a message;
- to provide information;
- to listen to concerns or the needs of stakeholders;
- to secure an informed decision;
- to gain agreement;
- to resolve differences of opinion;
- to get someone to take an action;
- to build a relationship.

And so on.

You might not consciously set the objective for an interaction with someone, especially if you happen to bump into them at the coffee machine. And not every interaction should be so calculated. It is OK to have a friendly conversation with a stakeholder without the objective of advancing your project in some way.

But for the actions you think through and consciously do with the goal of furthering your project, it is worth considering what you want the end result to be.

With your goal set, you can evaluate whether or not your engagement activity got the desired result.

Much of the time you'll quickly be able to see whether the engagement had the effect you were expecting. The stakeholder will take the decision, cascade information, approve a document, complete an action or whatever. There is tangible evidence that you've taken an action, influenced an individual and the result is that they have done something that equates to engagement with the project.

Engaging stakeholders on projects

Set time aside regularly to take stock of how engagement on the project is going. Monitor your results, even if you only do that informally, by yourself. It's simply an act of reflection. Ask:

- What did I do this week that engaged our key stakeholders?
- Did it work? Did they feel engaged? How do I know? Why do I think that?

Engaged stakeholders will tell you they've completed a task. You'll see if an action is taken. You'll use your emotional intelligence to pick up on whether the individual is feeling happy, confident and proud to be part of the project or whether they are annoyed that you are asking for their time and energy.

Reflecting will give you a gut feel for how some of those less tangible engagement actions are impacting the feedback and action you are seeing from the team.

Next, consider what you will do about what you've reflected on. If you feel confident that your engagement activities are having the desired effect, do more of what is working. If you have tried something and it didn't work, stop doing it. There's no point investing any more energy in that right now if you aren't seeing the benefits.

Adapt your approach as necessary. Table 3.4 shows some ways to adapt your engagement techniques to see what gives you the best response. Keep trying different things and see how individuals and groups respond.

You tried:	If you didn't get the results you hoped for	Try this:
Sending an email to get an action		Talk on the phone
Asking for feedback on a document		Book time to sit and go through it with them
Small group meeting		Individual meetings
Announcement on intranet		Desk drop of leaflets
Gaining commitment yourself		Use another person to influence
Sending minutes to confirm understanding		Allow time to discuss and circle back to summarise key decisions in next meeting
Conference call		Video conference
Sharing the vision in a conversation		Give a formal presentation

Table 3.4 Ways to change engagement approaches to test outcomes

You can also ask stakeholders how they feel about how the project is going, their contribution to the project and what could be done differently to make it easier for people to engage with the work.

Ask your questions and record the answers. Ask the same questions next month and see how the answers have changed. Hopefully, you will have taken action on the things they highlighted and you will be able to feed that back to them. Every time you ask, you'll be building a reputation as someone who cares about the experience of working on the project and about project success, as ultimately their feedback will only make it easier for the team to deliver something of value.[6]

People can get fatigued with only one source of communication or engagement so it's worth switching your actions up again in the future. Try something new, or repeat something that didn't work so well with a different group of stakeholders to see if you get better results next time. Keep testing what works and make changes accordingly.

If you are not seeing the levels of engagement you would like, try to shake up how you are interacting with people. Gamification is one way to do that.

Gamification

Gamification gets people to take action using the techniques and mechanics of games. APM research into gamification (2014) comments that:

Gamification techniques tap into and influence people's natural desires for competition, achievement, recognition and self-expression.

There are five principles from game mechanics that you can adopt in your stakeholder engagement to make it easier for people to want to get involved with a task or project.

---

[6] This question and answer format for tracking stakeholder satisfaction is the premise of *Customer-Centric Project Management*, a book I co-wrote with Phil Peplow. That book has a lot more detail in about how to measure and respond to stakeholder satisfaction and track project success during the project.

1. **Track your steps.** Many games provide a roadmap of levels to show you what you have achieved and where you are going next. You can do the same by creating a visual timeline for the project and using it frequently in communication to highlight which phase of the project you are talking about. Show people where they are in the journey to help them visualise progress, achievements and the plan.

2. **Take small actions.** Online games and social networks ask participants for small actions before big ones. You'll be asked to leave a review, share a status on a social network, like something or click something before being asked for larger engagements such as paying for access to a special game level. Get small engagements from stakeholders like asking them a yes/no question. Make it easy for them to take quick action with solutions like templated answers. Then ask for larger commitment.

3. **Create feedback loops.** Games tell you how you are doing. You have instant feedback on whether you've succeeded at a level or not, often with visual clues such as how many points you've earned. Give stakeholders the opportunity to provide immediate feedback (or as immediate as possible). Use surveys, forms, quizzes, lessons learned, retrospectives, stop/start/continue (see Appendix B), forums and chat channels and even pair people up to work on tasks together.

4. **Keep it simple.** The first few levels of a gaming app often walk you through core game features, perhaps creating your avatar or learning the controls. Keep things simple for your stakeholders. Stick to one message at a time,

A project to rollout a new computer system to 9,000 staff across more than 35 office locations was producing a lot of information about what the project meant to individuals, but it was hard to reach every member of staff. The project manager created a virtual scavenger hunt on the project's intranet site. She 'hid' a logo on 12 of the key intranet pages and set up a competition to find them via the project newsletter.

The challenge created a talking point for teams and also the opportunity for a photo call for the winner. The project manager bought a box of chocolates for the winner, who was drawn at random from the entries. While the contest didn't get hundreds of entries, it did encourage people who had not previously engaged with any of the communications to at least browse the intranet site.

asking for one action at a time. Don't assume prior knowledge about your project or the situation. Meet them where they are and provide what they need to know in order to progress. Checklists are great for this.

5. **Make it special.** Games celebrate your wins, however small, to encourage you to keep playing. Celebrate your project successes. Celebrate making progress. Celebrate the team's milestones such as birthdays or passing exams. Cultivate a fun environment for your project. Create a culture that people want to be part of.

Action steps

- Review your project/programme communications plan. Does it allow for tailoring and feedback loops? Are all stakeholders adequately reflected on the plan?
- Consider whether you are actively engaging core stakeholders in the project management process as well as the project deliverables. What could you share with them about project management that would make it easier for them to engage with the process?
- Pick a technique for engagement that is new to you and try it out.
- Review the five principles of gamification in a project environment. Pick one and use it in your next stakeholder engagement activity.

Key takeaways

- Project delivery professionals should be engaging stakeholders in the project management process as well as the deliverables/outcomes.
- Engagement is something that happens throughout the project life cycle.
- Anything that involves talking to or working with a stakeholder is an opportunity to engage – don't waste those moments.
- Tailor communication and engagement to meet the needs of the project and the stakeholders involved.

4

Facilitation and meetings

One of the big tools for engagement is talking to people, often in meetings either one-to-one or as a group. This chapter looks at techniques for running efficient meetings and facilitation. While there is a large body of literature around good techniques for doing both of those, this chapter pulls out key practical tips that you can start using today.

This chapter covers what facilitation is, how to facilitate a meeting with confidence and how to plan and deliver an effective meeting.

What is facilitation?

The *APM Body of Knowledge* defines facilitation as:

> *An approach to working with groups in a collaborative way to create energy and make it easy for the group to solve problems.*

In the role of facilitator, you take a neutral stance on the project, or in the meeting. You ask questions, foster participation, encourage creativity and let others lead from the floor. You are there to support the process whether that's problem solving, fact finding, brainstorming or something else. Your role as a facilitative leader is to help people get the result they need by managing the process.

Facilitation is exceptionally powerful in building engagement on projects. It helps people feel heard, ensures their contribution is understood and valued and creates ownership.

Facilitation is a skill that you can practice. It's a useful skill in situations beyond meetings because being a facilitator means asking the right questions, helping people stay engaged and creating an environment for work to get done effectively. Here are some examples of situations where a facilitative approach would be useful:

- **Project level:** Making connections between team members to enable them to work effectively together on project problems or tasks. Keeping the team motivated and engaged in delivery. Running risk workshops.

- **Programme level:** Creating a shared vision for the programme by facilitating discussions between different subject matter experts, owners and stakeholders. Reducing conflict. Running workshops relevant to the programme.
- **Portfolio level:** Facilitating a common understanding of how inflight and pipeline projects can support the delivery of strategy. Ensuring buy in and support for the change management activities required across the organisation. Consider different options before moving ahead with executing a strategic plan.

While facilitation skills can be used in a variety of settings, it is easiest to describe them in the context of a meeting. When you have gained confidence facilitating groups, you'll find it easy to use the same skills in one-to-one conversations to get the best out of an individual's performance.

Ultimately, facilitation skills become baked into the way you work as a project manager. With experience, you'll be able to step up and lead as required, or step back and facilitate if that's what the project needs from you at any given moment.

Using a neutral facilitator

Many project managers today find themselves being one of the people doing work on the project, as well as fulfilling the project management role. Your subject matter expertise, or simply lack of resources across the organisation, might mean that you also have a 'doing' role to play on the project, as well as your role coordinating the work.

When you have a stake in decision-making, it is harder to take the neutral stance of a facilitator. In this situation, you may be best served by having someone else come into your project meeting to facilitate the session on your behalf. You can then focus fully on engaging and participating, sharing your subject matter or task expertise.

A neutral facilitator could be another project or programme manager, or an individual from the Project Management Office. In-house resources are often good at running facilitated meetings as they will likely know the people involved. The project team will feel comfortable with a colleague in the room and you can explain why you have brought in someone else to run the session.

Alternatively, you can buy in the support of an external facilitator. This could be worth the investment for particularly difficult workshops, where you are expecting conflict, workshops that are scheduled for at least a whole day.

Whether you use an internal or external facilitator, expect to spend some time with them, briefing them on the goals and objectives for the session, helping them understand the personalities who will be present and going through the agenda in detail. All meetings are more effective when the session is properly prepared. Even if you are not in the chair on the day, as the project manager you still have a role to play in ensuring the meeting is adequately prepared so it can be run effectively.

Running a successful meeting

There are many different types of meeting that you will use on a project including:

- group discovery sessions;
- kick off meetings;
- requirements elicitation meetings;
- status meetings;
- meetings focused on key project management topics such as budget or risk management;
- urgent problem-solving meetings;
- workshops;
- retrospectives and lessons learned sessions;
- project closure meetings.

The exact agenda, invitees and expected outcomes will differ depending on what objectives you have for the meeting. Different types of meeting will require different steps for planning. A virtual meeting, for example, requires you to set up the tech to enable everyone to join the web conference.

However, there are common types of preparation for any meeting. Being prepared will help you get the best outcome from the meeting and make the best use of everyone's time.

The section below looks at what to do before, during and after the meeting to ensure your session is effective.

Before the meeting

The work to ensure any meeting will be effective happens before the meeting takes place. Here are some activities to do prior to the meeting to get the best out of the time.

Engaging stakeholders on projects

- Define the objective: why are you bringing people together? Can you achieve the same objective without a meeting?
- Decide who should attend. Aim to have as few people in the room as possible, but make sure attendees have the right level of authority to be able to contribute and make decisions.
- Decide on the location. Book a meeting room if you need one, or set up a web conference. Sort out any other logistics requirements such as equipment for the room and refreshments.
- Prepare an agenda. Depending on the type of meeting, you may want to solicit input to the agenda from the attendees before you publish it. If you are nominating someone else to speak on a topic, make sure they agree and are prepared to lead that part of the conversation during the meeting. Make sure breaks are factored into the agenda if the session is more than two hours.
- Prepare any other meeting papers e.g. status update reports, presentations. Get hold of updates or papers you need from other participants.
- Send out the meeting invite including time and date, location, and agenda to attendees. Attach any documentation or reports that will be discussed in the meeting so people have a chance to review the materials in advance. If you expect them to make time to read the papers before the meeting, state that there will not be time during the meeting allocated to review the content, so please come prepared. You can also redistribute the minutes from the last meeting if they are relevant to this meeting.
- Socialise your ideas i.e. start talking informally to people about the topics that will be discussed in the meeting. This is particularly relevant if decisions are going to be made in the meeting and you want attendees to have had adequate time to think through your proposals.
- Make copies of essential documents as back up in case your tech fails on the day e.g. have a separate copy of your presentation emailed to yourself or a colleague, print a copy etc.
- Confirm the room booking the day before. If you regularly have people fail to attend meetings, email or call participants and remind them of the meeting and why it is important they attend.

Prepare in advance

There are a lot of preparatory tasks in the list above, and it may feel overkill for a chat with some colleagues. However, facilitated meetings take more preparation than a typical project status meeting or standup that you run regularly. You need to think through how to get the best out of the time and what process you want to use to foster discussion and debate.

Prepare questions to ask about each topic. Make sure you have your notes with you on the day. Let the discussion flow, but be prepared to bring it back on topic with an interjection or question to keep the group moving forward.

Prepare your activities too. For example, if you are starting the meeting with a group ice-breaker exercise, know what you are going to say, what materials you need, how long you are able to allocate to the activity and how you are going to bring it to a close (will you need a bell or similar to get the attention of everyone in the room?).

You tend to use more resources in facilitated sessions than you would in a regular project meeting. Make sure you've got the flip chart paper, pens, sticky notes, or online environment set up the way you want it so you are ready to go with your activities.

Kim Wasson writes about planning the meeting to cater for different learning styles in her book, *The Socially Intelligent Project Manager: Soft Skills That Prevent Hard Days*. She identifies five learning styles:

1. Visual.
2. Reading.
3. Auditory.
4. Tactile.
5. Kinetic.

Make sure visual learners have something to look at, like a whiteboard, graphs or pictures. People with a reading preference will engage with handouts or when there are words on the screen – and you can count on them to have read the materials you've circulated in advance. Auditory learners want to hear you talk about a topic, so prepare a short summary of the topic. Bring paper copies of the agenda for tactile learners. Tell everyone it's OK to stretch and walk around (if it is OK) so that those with a kinetic preference can engage while moving.

Small nods to people's different working styles will help everyone engage with the meeting in the way that feels best for them.

The more prepared you are, the more professional you'll look and people will respond to you accordingly. You'll also have more confidence knowing that you're well-prepared.

Keep the meeting small

It is easier to facilitate discussions with smaller groups. The logistics are simpler when there are fewer people talking. You can more easily make sure everyone has the opportunity to participate and manage the noise level in the room during breakout conversations.

Meetings with fewer people also tend to be shorter, which is a good thing.

Ideally, you are after a 'Goldilocks' situation in your meeting: not too few people as otherwise you wouldn't be able to get any decisions made, not too many people, as that creates delay and bloats the meeting. You want just the right amount of people.

Research by Marcia W. Blenko, Michael C. Mankins and Paul Rogers, for their book, *Decide & Deliver: 5 Steps to Breakthrough Performance in Your Organization*, shows that once you've got seven people in a decision-making group, each additional member reduces decision effectiveness by 10 per cent.

Don't invite anyone who won't add value. If all the 'value add' people push the number of attendees above seven, then think about what decisions you need to get made and whether this meeting is the right forum to achieve them.

Establish credibility before the meeting

People respond best to a colleague who has already demonstrated themselves as credible. You can do this without ever having had any interaction with others. Simply start out on a professional footing by booking the meeting in plenty of time, sending a professional, comprehensive agenda and being clear on what the session is for. This sends the message that you are organised and have no intention of wasting anyone's time.

What if you can't plan?

Ideally, you should have some time before any workshop or meeting to think about what you want to get out of it to make the best use of everyone's time.

But sometimes you won't get the opportunity to do the planning you would like.

For example, your boss comes over to your desk and asks you to come into a meeting that's already in progress, or requests that you get everyone together *right now* for a discussion about a particular issue. Maybe a meeting you are already in takes a different turn and your project sponsor agrees that you can veer off into a brainstorming session on something totally different to the original meeting topic.

In those cases, you're going to have to cope the best you can. The more meetings you attend and facilitate, the easier it will be. Over time, you learn what works best for your personal style and the group you are leading, especially if you work with a core team over some time.

Try to take a confident lead on the discussion. Create opportunities for everyone to have their say. Acknowledge (to yourself) that this might not be the best meeting you've ever chaired, but do the best you can. Take a moment to reflect after the meeting and consider how you felt you did: it might have gone better than you were expecting.

During the meeting

Being an effective meeting chair takes practice and is a skill you can work at. Here are some considerations for during the meeting.

Managing stress

Chairing a meeting and facilitating can feel like very stressful moments in the day, but they don't have to be. Part of the stress comes from feeling in the spotlight. As the person 'in charge' in the room, it can feel like all eyes are on you.

That doesn't have to be the case. Good facilitators keep the focus on the group. They are there to manage the process and to encourage the group to stick to the agenda and timelines set. Whether you are facilitating a workshop or chairing a small meeting, you are there to serve the needs of the group and support them in finding a way to achieve the objectives of the meeting.

There will be some cases where you will need to stand at the front of a room and deliver a presentation, but again, it's only to serve a need for the group. The right mindset and good preparation will help you combat meeting-related stress.

Another tip: before you enter the meeting room, take a moment to compose yourself, breathe deeply and then open the door with a smile.

Own the room

Own the room is another way of saying lead the meeting with confidence. It's your meeting. Even if you are not there to participate or give your opinion, as the facilitator, the attendees should be looking to you to set the tone and monitor acceptable behaviour.

When people enter the meeting space for the first time, go up to them (in person, or virtually), introduce yourself and establish yourself as the meeting facilitator.

Think about your body language and make eye contact with participants during the session.

Have a few phrases planned in advance to use to shut down interruptions or keep the meeting moving forward. You could use phrases like these:

- "I'll come back to you in a moment, but for now, can we let [name] finish their point?"
- "That sounds like an important point, but it's not a topic we have time for today. I'll add it to the parking lot. Can we continue on the theme of [topic]?"
- "Can I remind everyone of the ground rules we agreed to?" You don't need to name and shame anyone – simply draw the group's attention back to the ground rules and move on. Ground rules are discussed in the contracting section below.
- "That sounds like something we should be discussing in more detail, but we could run out of time if we go into it now. We've got some options. What do you think? Shall we dive into this topic or put it on the parking lot?"
- "Does anyone have any comments or thoughts on [name]'s point before we move on?"

Practice saying the phrases out loud before the meeting.

Interruptions can be collaborative (the interruption supports the point being made) or intrusive (the interruption disrupts the conversation or changes the topic). You'll use different strategies for each type, so be prepared to flex your responses and style depending on how the meeting is going.

Contracting at the start of a meeting

The most useful tool for successful facilitation, in my experience, is careful contracting with the meeting participants. This basically means setting expectations for what the meeting is for, who is going to do what, how you intend to work together and what will happen after the meeting.

As people settle into their chairs and you formally open the discussion, take a few minutes to run through these points:

The goal of this meeting is . . .

State the objective(s) of the meeting. Ideally, have this visible on a piece of flip chart paper tacked to the wall, or shown at the top of the screen for virtual meetings.

Frame the objectives as statements of things you want to achieve by the end of the meeting, e.g. to come up with a plan for dealing with a particular risk, to create a first draft of our high-level timeline, to brainstorm suggestions for ways to fix an issue, to gain clarity on who's doing what in Phase 2 etc.

Today, we're going to cover . . .

Briefly outline the agenda for the day, highlighting when you have scheduled breaks and – if the meeting goes over lunch – what the food plans are.

These people are helping run the session . . .

People will already have worked out that you are the facilitator, but say it again if you feel that it warrants calling out. Also name the person doing the timekeeping and the meeting scribe, if you have them.

Facilitated workshops should have someone keeping an eye on the time and someone else available to take notes, so you can fully focus on facilitation. In practice, you might not have extra hands available to you so plan for how you are going to do all the roles if you have to. If you have not been able to organise someone from the group to take on these roles before the meeting, you can always ask for a volunteer to help keep time or scribe at this point. They aren't onerous jobs and you might find someone in the group willing to help.

Let's think about the ground rules for this session . . .

If appropriate, talk about ground rules for interaction and discussion as a group. Ground rules tend to be useful for larger groups coming together for the first time, or for sessions where there is likely to be heated discussion or brainstorming. They set the tone for how the meeting will run and clarify behaviour guidelines for how the group will interact. You will not need to discuss ground rules in established teams.

Ground rules include:

- Make sure you are on time returning from breaks.
- Be present: do not use your laptop or phone in the meeting room.
- Practice active listening and do not speak over other people.
- Make sure everyone has a turn to express their ideas.
- Challenge the idea, not the person.

Let the participants come up with the ground rules themselves; you are more likely to get buy in that way than if you show a pre-prepared list of rules. However, make sure your agenda leaves enough time for a discussion about the ground rules so that agreement can be reached.

Because of the time it takes to set ground rules effectively, you might choose not to encourage discussion in shorter meetings. Instead say something like: "As always, I'd encourage you to be on time returning from breaks because we have a lot to get through. If you need to take a call, we all know sometimes it's important, just pop out and do so."

We'll be capturing actions as we go. . .

Tell people how the follow up will work. Say that you will be capturing actions, owners and deadlines during the meeting and will send out a consolidated list of tasks.

Hopefully, all of this will be already known to the meeting attendees. It's a good idea to brief everyone on the purpose of the meeting before they arrive so they can properly prepare. Aim for no surprises during this section of the meeting and you'll find you can get through contracting quite quickly.

Plan a response if conflict arises

Even the most supportive, well-established teams sometimes face conflict. Facilitated meetings are one of the places where this conflict can arise. You're often dealing with new ideas, establishing project requirements or trying to agree the way forward about a tricky problem. It's normal that people will have different thoughts about the best approach or what should be done next.

Given that conflict is almost certainly going to arise at some point, part of your preparation should be considering what to do when it does.

There is more about conflict management and resolution in Chapter 6.

Managing interruptions and multi-taskers

There are two schools of thought about people multi-tasking in meetings via taking calls or checking emails.

The 'old school' approach is that you should encourage meeting participants to turn their phones to silent and focus fully on the meeting discussion. People who check their emails during a meeting are frowned at and their lack of attention commented on in hushed voices after the meeting.

However, in my experience, the higher up the organisation you go, the more likely it is that people will be reluctant to put down their phones for a couple of hours to give you their full attention. When the CEO rings, you don't send the call to voicemail. There is a hierarchy of attention and often your project does not trump the person on the end of the line.

There's also increasing urgency with certain jobs. For example, I've been in meetings with clinical staff who have got up and walked out of a project planning meeting as they were needed at a patient's bedside. What's more important in a hospital, patient care or an IT project meeting? It's hardly a difficult call.

I remember the days when no one took a laptop into a meeting room. These days, many people do. They have a digital copy of the agenda, presentation and past minutes. They might be taking their own notes on the device during the meeting. You might want your scribe to be typing notes into a minutes template or your action log to save time transcribing from paper later. It's hard to give the message that it's OK for you to have your laptop open so you can show the slide deck, but no one else is allowed to bring their device into the room.

Of course, when an attendee has got their laptop open, they *are* going to flick over to check their inbox whenever the subject matter veers from their area of expertise or when they see the notification that a new message has come in. The fear of leaving a three-hour workshop and returning to an inbox full of 50+ messages is real.

When your subject matter experts are senior leaders with complex jobs in a fast-moving environment, and they don't have the back up of someone else who can fully cover for them during your meeting time, then you need to be prepared for people to sit attached to their devices.

Coping with information overload

When you aren't the subject matter expert in the room, a lot of what is discussed in a project meeting may sound like a different language. The first few weeks of a project are normally particularly overwhelming as you get up to speed with a new topic and a new set of experts to work with.

Even if you know nothing about the topic, you can still add value as a facilitator and as a project manager.

Absorb as much information as you can during the meeting. In a few months, maybe sooner, you'll be speaking this language too, but first you have to go through the learning curve.

Ask questions. Phrase back what you are hearing to the speaker, to check you have understood. Interrupt politely and ask for clarification or to ask a follow up question. Take notes as you go. If you don't feel you can constantly interrupt, keep a running list of terms and abbreviations you don't understand and ask about them afterwards.

Try to structure the information for your personal benefit and that of the others in the room. Aim to create a big picture view of what they are sharing. Look for patterns and groupings. Elevate what you can to the highest possible level and simplify.

Think about what you can do with the information. Bring the discussion to a pause and reflect for a moment. Ask them what they think the next steps are. Ask if anyone else needs to know about what they have discussed or decided.

Finally, documenting decisions and actions is always a value-add in a meeting. Don't underestimate the benefit that structure brings to a group of experts. Say, "How do you want me to phrase that action in the minutes?" if you don't know what they are talking about.

Other considerations during a meeting

Here are some final considerations for ensuring your meeting goes well:

- At the beginning of the meeting, introduce people who do not yet know each other. Introduce yourself to people you don't know – don't wait for them to come up to you.
- Briefly reiterate why you are all together and the purpose of the meeting. Outline the core agenda topics to clarify what will be discussed. Ask if anyone has any other business. If they do, make a note to leave enough time at the end of the meeting to discuss their points.
- Set up a space, such as a flip chart sheet tacked to the wall or a blank open document, to record topics that are worthy of discussion but are not tabled for debate today. This is your 'parking lot'. Use it during the meeting to note down subjects to which the team needs to return at a future point. One of your actions at the end of the meeting will be to clear the parking lot, by setting up future times to discuss those items.
- Follow the agenda, ensuring everyone has the chance to participate actively in discussions.
- Take notes for the minutes, or assign someone else to be the note taker.
- Record any actions as they come up, along with who will be responsible for working on them and when the action will be completed.
- Close the meeting on time, thanking participants for their involvement and arranging a time for a follow up meeting if necessary.

After the meeting

The work of the meeting chair does not stop when the attendees leave the meeting room. You still have work to do to ensure any actions are carried forward. Here are some activities to focus on once your meeting is over:

- Leave the meeting room as you found it. Make sure to remove any confidential material or notes, including those left behind by attendees.
- If you had a guest speaker or subject matter expert from an external organisation, get in touch to thank them for attending.
- Write up the minutes. Get the minutes validated/checked if necessary and issue them to attendees within a week, preferably within 48 hours.

- Call anyone who didn't attend to brief them on key points.
- Update your project documentation with any actions, risks, decisions, issues, schedule changes etc. that came out of the meeting.
- Complete your own actions.
- Follow up with other people as required to make sure they complete actions allocated to them. Many people appreciate a quick check in or reminder about their actions before the next meeting, so if they have forgotten, they have the opportunity to complete their work before being asked about it in the group. Informal check ins are also a good way to reassure yourself that work is progressing as planned on the project.

Virtual meetings

Much of the advice for successfully running in-person meetings is the same for virtual meetings. You want to set objectives for the session, introduce participants to each other, have an agenda, work through the topics, start and finish on time.

But virtual meetings somehow feel more complicated. It's true that facilitating an online meeting does involve slightly different skills as you can't see the people in the 'room' to engage with them.

A virtual meeting timetabled for more than two hours is going to be a challenge. It is hard to keep people engaged for that long as the meeting chair. It's hard to concentrate for that long as an attendee.

Aim to keep your virtual meetings short and to the point. If you need a lot of time with people, schedule multiple smaller meetings, or at least plan plenty of scheduled breaks in your online day.

"Successful virtual leaders need to act as the connector for the people on their team," writes Nancy Settle-Murphy in her book, *Leading Effective Virtual Teams*.

Encourage the team to connect before your meeting so they have the opportunity to build relationships with each other outside of the formal meeting setting. That can also make the meeting shorter, as they will have already had the chance to discuss important topics.

You'll probably find it easier to engage your stakeholders face-to-face, but you won't always be able to do that. Try to choose the highest-touch option for your virtual interactions. A one-to-one phone call creates more engagement than a conference call with 20 people on the line. A web conference with video is more engaging than a call without video.

Whatever tech you use, always test it in advance and make sure you are confident driving it. If you can, opt for a wired network connection over wifi and try to be in a place with a stable connection and good phone signal.

Action steps

- Review the agendas you use regularly. Is there scope for a refresh to make them even more focused and useful?
- Have a colleague video you facilitating a meeting or giving a presentation. Watch the video back and review your body language. Is your personal presence sending the confident messages you want it to? What would be more effective?
- Pick one or two of the further reading books dedicated to facilitation in the Bibliography. Read more on the topic and then choose an element to focus on, building up your skills in that area.

Key takeaways

- Facilitation is an approach to working with groups in a collaborative way to create energy and make it easy for the group to solve problems.
- Confident facilitation in meetings relies on credibility, preparation and the ability to help the group stay with the process while limiting your own personal influence on the discussion and outcomes.
- Get the best results from a meeting with full preparation beforehand, strong leadership during the meeting and a professional follow up.

5

Dealing with resistance to engagement

Projects and programmes change things. And not everyone embraces change.

This chapter looks at how to identify resistance to engagement and why it happens. It covers practical techniques to engage with people who are resistant to your project work.

There is no guarantee the techniques will work on your stakeholders, but hopefully the advice in this chapter will give you a solid grounding in simple approaches to try to turn around behaviour where you can.

How to identify resistance to engagement

Sometimes it is obvious to see which stakeholders are unsupportive of your work: your stakeholder analysis will have identified them earlier. Sometimes they'll come right out and tell you that they don't support the project or they are resistant to the change because of the impact it will have on them or their team.

However, some stakeholders are better at disguising their lack of support than others. Here's what to look for if you suspect someone of being covertly resistant to your efforts to engage them on the project:

- Stakeholders who accept meeting invites but then don't show up, or who turn up so late that they aren't able to make a meaningful contribution.
- Stakeholders who accept meeting invites but then send someone in their place who does not have the delegated authority to be useful.
- Stakeholders who sit silently through meetings and make no contribution (although before writing this person off as unsupportive, probe to see if they are uncomfortable contributing in a meeting environment for some reason).
- Stakeholders who don't reply to emails or return phone calls.
- Stakeholders who don't have time to come to briefing sessions or to learn more about the project, but who do have the time to complain about the project to anyone who will listen.

Engaging stakeholders on projects

- Stakeholders who don't complete their actions and have no good reason why.
- Stakeholders who promise to share information with their team and then you find out they never did, even though they had the opportunity.
- Stakeholders who do not deliver the things they committed to do.
- Stakeholders who question the project management process or the way the change is being delivered, for example, by asking for other subject matter experts to review the solution, querying why certain tools are being used over others etc. They do not question the project deliverables, but are picking holes where they can.

All of these can apply to core project team members as well as those individuals you might more traditionally think of as stakeholders.

These, and you can probably think of more, are all signs of someone who is not fully committed to project success for some reason. When these things happen, project timelines and budgets are adversely affected. The team's motivation can also be affected, because it feels as if they are constantly pushing and not receiving support for their work. Longer term, project benefits are affected because lack of support can mean that the full scope is not delivered in the expected way, or that the deliverables are not fully used to their full advantage.

Why people resist change

People resist change for lots of reasons including:

- they are scared;
- they are unwilling – consciously or unconsciously – to make the effort to change;
- they don't understand the benefits or they don't think there will be any;
- they can't see an advantage to them if the project is completed;
- they can see a disadvantage to them if the project is completed;
- they are unhappy about the personal implications of the project e.g. they are going to be made redundant;
- they don't understand about why the project or change is happening and therefore do not give it the priority it requires;
- they are part of your virtual team but located in the same building as their manager or other colleagues, and those people get their attention first;

- they have had previous poor experience of how projects and change were managed;
- the organisation (or another organisation they have worked in) has a history of talking about delivery but nothing actually getting done so they don't believe it's worth investing the time in this work as it will come to nothing;
- they have come to the project late e.g. as the result of a scope change, and aren't yet fully invested in the outcome;
- they don't like you (or the project sponsor) enough to want to make any effort to engage.

Resistance to change can also come from a place of positivity. A stakeholder could genuinely have a reason for being nervous about fully committing to this project. Engaging with that person could uncover risks or challenges you were not previously aware of, and that will help shape the direction of the project.

One of the top reasons why people are resistant to change is that they weren't involved earlier. This causes problems for project teams because you've got dates you've committed to. Now you can't achieve them because a stakeholder isn't supportive of the work you need to get done. Perhaps they are asking for additional briefings before they commit their team to some work, or they are querying the solution you've already had agreed by the project board.

If you're in that situation, you'll need to do the best you can to get through it quickly, dealing with their resistance so that the project can get moving again.

Next time though, schedule your project after you've done at least some engaging.

Resistance to change is a normal and natural response. Jonah Berger, in his book *The Catalyst*, writes that people tend to do what they've always done. He adds:

> Whether trying to change company culture or get the kids to eat their vegetables, the assumption is that pushing harder will do the trick. That if we just provide more information, more facts, more reasons, more arguments, or just add a little more force, people will change.
>
> Implicitly, this approach assumes that people are like marbles. Push them in one direction and they will go that way.
>
> Unfortunately, that approach often backfires. Unlike marbles, people don't just roll with it when you try to push them. They push back. Rather than saying

yes, the client stops returning our calls. Rather than going along, the boss says they'll think about it, which is a nice way of saying "Thanks, but no way."

As individuals, we understand the status quo and how we fit into that. Change equals upheaval, and often it's upheaval because of someone else's agenda for the business, not our own.

This can make the early engagement conversations more challenging, but even more important to have. And remember, someone's engagement levels can drop through the life of the project: it's not just at the beginning that you need to look out for resistance.

Resistance is wider than you think

If you've picked up on the body language or actions of one colleague and realised that they aren't fully supportive and engaging with the change, then the chances are there are more people out there who feel the same way. They're just better at hiding it.

Don't assume that because you can only see a few pockets of reluctance to change that there are only a few pockets.

If one individual or team is showing signs of being disengaged, then there is a high likelihood other people have similar feelings, to a greater or lesser extent. Perhaps they haven't had the opportunity to raise it with you, or they are worried about the repercussions if they do. Perhaps there are other reasons why it hasn't yet come to your attention. These quiet individuals will find their voice at some point. It will be better for the project if they do so sooner rather than later.

When you notice resistance to change, please assume that it stretches wider than you can see. Plan your change management activities and engagement actions with that in mind. If you're right, you'll be able to address multiple project detractors at the same time. If you're lucky and there isn't a wider unrest bubbling under the surface, then you've strengthened your engagement anyway.

Dealing with resistant stakeholders takes time. This is yet one more reason why you should plan time for engaging with people. Don't assume you can squeeze some communications or engagement into your day. Carve out regular time for it.

Engaging resisters

Don't worry if you encounter some resistance to change in your early discussions with stakeholders. That is what engagement is for. Over time, and as you build a relationship with them, you should be able to influence their opinion and actions related to the project to shift them towards becoming more supportive.

However, you might come across people who resist more stubbornly – people who aren't open to engaging with you or the project. Your efforts so far have not been successful and you aren't able to get these people involved in the project in the way you would like.

This is actually a positive thing: now you know who they are. Going forward you can plan your next steps to more fully understand their position and influence their actions.

There are a range of options available to you to try to engage resistant stakeholders. They won't all work, so pick the tactic from the list below that you think is going to have the best result . . . and if it doesn't work, try something else.

Don't be difficult to work with

Stakeholders are busy people.

Minimise the distractions for them. Keep meeting notes and communications short. Make clear requests. Be efficient and easy to work with so they don't have to think too much about what you are really asking.

Provide a terms of reference document for their involvement, or a roles and responsibilities document setting out what is needed from them. Ideally, you would work on this with them, but over-stretched stakeholders sometimes value simply being told what to do. They want to buy into the project, but don't have the capacity to engage fully. If you are clear in your requests, they are happy to comply, but they don't want to spend too much time engaging for the sake of it. Documenting expectations will help you both in this situation.

If someone is reluctant to engage because doing so is too time-consuming or requires too much brain power, then this might be all they need to participate again.

Be realistic with your expectations

How important is your project, really?

Project managers who expect senior stakeholders engaged with strategic initiatives to drop everything to respond to a question about a small process change are going to be sadly disappointed. You aren't going to get the Chief Finance Officer's attention during the year end preparation of the accounts, for example.

Let's be realistic: not every project is big and strategically important. Even the relatively small stuff needs a project manager and that could be you. Sometimes other projects take priority. Sometimes it's the rhythm and flow of the business that takes priority over project work that is perceived to be less important: closing a strategically significant deal, preparing for the announcement of financial results to city analysts, and so on.

Apply commercial awareness to your dealings with reluctant stakeholders. Are they genuinely fully engaged on other things that have a higher priority than your work? If so, you either have to find a way to increase the perceived priority of your project, or accept that you're always going to be scrabbling around for crumbs of their time. If the latter, think carefully about what you need to engage them with so you make the best use of the attention they can give you. And if they are crucial stakeholders with no opportunity to engage, then recommend the project is postponed until they are available to support the work.

Acknowledge you've noticed

Be open with them. Say you've picked up that they aren't supportive of the change (add in concrete evidence of their behaviour if you have it) and you would like to find out more about that. If that feels too confrontational, ask the same thing as a question: "There was something I wanted to ask you. I thought you sounded a little reluctant about [insert specific action or topic] in our meeting earlier on and I wondered if I was reading that right?" Then pause.

Once they have responded, offer to help them with whatever the issue is. If they say there isn't an issue, you can make a generic offer of help.

They might shift their behaviour solely on the basis that someone has noticed they aren't following the corporate line.

Note: don't call them out on their lack of support in front of anyone else. This is a strategy for your one-to-one meetings. It's easier to have this conversation as an aside to another conversation. You might feel more confident if the main purpose of your meeting is another topic, and you bring up their lack of support almost as an afterthought.

Listen

Really listen. Make the time to hear what's being said.

You will be better placed to address concerns if you understand what they are concerned about.

In particular, transformation projects and wide-scale reformation of how projects are managed, such as in creating or reforming a PMO, can cause more anxiety than smaller projects. People typically have experience of 'normal' projects and 'normal' change. Transformation initiatives – anything labelled as 'strategic' – feel more unsettling because the stakes are higher for the organisation, the projects have oversight at a much more senior level, and the level of disruption and change might not yet be fully understood, even by the delivery team.

But don't assume you know why people feel the way they do. Ask for and listen to feedback. Try to get to the underlying reasons for any anxiety or reluctance to change.

As you listen and observe them, you might realise that they are generally negative and unsupportive of all initiatives, not only your project. That piece of information will help you frame your engagement activities going forward.

Finally on this topic, remember that people's opinions change over time. Don't ever stop listening. As stakeholders find out more about the project, the strategy and what it means to them, their views evolve and that could be a positive or negative thing for your engagement approach.

There are more tips to build your active listening skills in Chapter 7.

Ask for their help

It's hard to say no to someone asking for help because of the social pressures and conventions that constrain our environment and organisational culture. Plus, it's flattering to think that someone needs our help.

People like to think their opinion matters. If this person is worthy of spending time trying to engage them on the project even though they are showing resistance, then their opinion really does matter.

A simple way to ask for help is to ask their opinion on how the project is going. Ask whether they could pinpoint anything that could be done differently to better engage their team or colleagues, or to develop the solution more quickly or whatever their subject matter area is.

If they do provide some feedback, act on it where you can and then follow up with them to say how grateful you were for the suggestion and tell them what you have done about it.

Slowly, these small interactions may win over a resistant stakeholder.

Thank them

Mention them in conversations with others, praising them (or their team) for the contribution they've made to the project so far. The reluctant stakeholder doesn't even have to be in the room for this (although it can help). The office grapevine will normally ensure that praise gets back to the person being praised.

Of course, they have to have done something in order to merit praise. If they haven't, you could talk about how much you are looking forward to working with them and how much you value the contribution you know their area is going to make.

When other people expect certain behaviour – because they've been told the stakeholder will be contributing in a valuable way – it's harder to back out of delivering on those promises. It's also flattering to be praised. Use this technique sparingly and on the individuals you feel will respond best to a bit of ego massaging.

Go via the gatekeeper

Some stakeholders may be hard to get hold off. Think about how you can best reach them. Sometimes the best technique is to go via their 'gatekeeper' instead of directly. Gatekeepers are the guardians of their diaries and inboxes. That could be an executive assistant, personal assistant or equivalent.

Make friends with the person who controls access to the stakeholder. That's a good tip even for stakeholders who aren't reluctant to engage. Be professional, polite and clear with your requests. Acknowledge their position and the value they add to their manager. They've probably come across plenty of people who have dismissed them as 'only' a secretary: don't be one of them.

Don't make things worse

Let's take the case of redundancy. While some employees may be happy to take a payout and move on to another company, others are simply never going to positively engage with the project. They'll engage because they have to, but they will do so unwillingly.

If you come across stakeholders in this kind of situation, the judicious and appropriate thing would be to acknowledge the situation and not expend effort trying to shift their behaviour to making a positive, proactive contribution. Some employees may make that shift of their own accord, but sometimes the best you can do is not make things feel worse for people.

Plan your engagement activities to be precise, timely, honest and clear so that everyone knows where they stand.

Persuade with data and stories

Different individuals respond to different inputs. Perhaps you haven't yet found the best way to interact with this particular stakeholder. If you've already tried data, try a customer story. If you've tried to engage with emotion, try facts.

If you've already explained the corporate project benefits, explain what it means to them and their team as a division or as individuals. Or vice versa: some people are motivated by seeing the bigger picture and understanding how important this initiative is to supporting company goals.

> The words you choose have a huge impact on the success (or otherwise) of your ability to influence someone. In his book, *Exactly What To Say: The Magic Words for Influence and Impact*, Phil M. Jones sets out lots of examples of how you can shift behaviour with small tweaks to the way you phrase a request. For example:
>
> > "What do you know about . . ." is a way to uncover the precise cause of their resistance. It opens the door for you to provide additional information where the stakeholder has gaps in their knowledge.
> >
> > "When would be a good time . . ." presupposes that there will be a good time to discuss the project with them and leads you into a conversation about finding that time.
> >
> > "Do you have any questions?" is a closed question that prompts for a yes/no answer. Switching that to "What questions do you have for me?" is a better way to encourage dialogue.

Escalate

Sometimes the best course of action is to share your concerns with the project sponsor or someone else senior to you. Those individuals who have set the direction for the project may have ideas about how to engage reluctant stakeholders. It's also helpful for them to hear about the resistance you are facing on the project.

If nothing else, a senior stakeholder may be able to influence the reluctant stakeholder in a way that you are unable to do. Your sponsor could have a conversation with them about the rationale and strategic importance of the project. That discussion may influence the level to which the stakeholder is prepared to engage.

Ignore them

Ignoring them is an option, but one to use with care. Consider the relative power and influence of a stakeholder and then decide how much effort you need to expend on someone who is resistant to the changes you are trying to put through.

For example, if an individual team member in a functional team is unsupportive of the project, but their team leader is fully onboard, you could step back from that disengagement and let the team leader handle the situation.

Jake Holloway, David Bryde and Roger Joby have written extensively about dealing with challenging colleagues. In their book, *A Practical Guide to Dealing with Difficult Stakeholders*, they offer some additional tactics for managing conversations with difficult people.

They suggest exposing people who say one thing and do another by keeping detailed notes. Then you can call out their unacceptable behaviour and back yourself up with evidence.

They also suggest entrapping stakeholders by forcing them to either support or dismiss your project in a public setting, such as endorsing a plan. If everyone else in the room supports the plan, it becomes more of a challenge for the difficult stakeholder to say publicly that they don't support the plan.

However, neither of these tactics are particularly engaging. They work, and you might be able to navigate a difficult conversation more easily, but you aren't building long-term engagement, so use them with care.

Stakeholder risk

Disengaged stakeholders present project risk. People risk is just as important to your project as risks caused by other factors, but project teams tend not to write people risks down because they can be highly sensitive.

Whether you choose to document stakeholder risks or not is up to you, but you should at least reflect on the impact people could have to your project, programme or portfolio.

Think about:

- Who could stop this project from meeting the success criteria?
- Who could make this project a roaring success?
- How are people going to feel about the changes this project or programme is going to deliver?
- What would happen if stakeholders did not stay on top of their project tasks? How could we re-engage them to keep them on track with delivery?
- What can we do to address those feelings (where the feelings are negative) or encourage those feelings (where the feelings are positive)?

A further risk to any project where stakeholders are not fully engaged from Day 1 (which is all of them) is that behaviour change takes time. Plan enough time to affect behaviour change and try to ensure that when the project closes, there is still a support structure in place to encourage and reinforce the changes that have been made. Whether it's a large-scale business transformation, or using the new features in an incremental software release, your project work asks people to do something different. Getting used to that takes time. Plan for it.

Moving beyond resistance

Identifying and acting on resistance is something you will do throughout the project. It means communicating more frequently and more readily than perhaps you initially planned to do.

Keep the communication channels open, even when you think the stakeholder is ready to engage positively with the project.

Moving forward, you will hopefully be able to spend less time on engaging reluctant stakeholders and more on forward-looking engagement activities, preparing the stakeholder community for the project deliverables and the resulting change.

However, remember that disengagement can happen at any time, for any reason, and you should always be on the lookout for changes in stakeholder behaviour that could signal a drop in engagement levels.

Typically, there's unspoken conflict between stakeholders who support the work and stakeholders who don't. And conflict is something that can be managed, facilitated and resolved because the tools are available to do that. These are discussed in Chapter 6.

Action steps

- Review your stakeholder analysis. Who have you identified as potentially resistant to engage? Pick a technique to try to re-engage them with the project.
- Introduce yourself to the gatekeepers for your executive stakeholders. Remember their names and, if you can, their birthdays. Put Administrative Professionals Day in your diary and pop by their desk with a box of chocolates or similar when it comes around.
- Plan a time to talk to a particularly difficult stakeholder. Think about what you want to get out of the discussion and book a meeting with them to start the conversation. Remember, it might be easier for you both if the meeting is ostensibly about something else and your engagement conversation is a subsidiary point.

Key takeaways

- Not everyone is going to support your project – but you knew that already, right?
- There are a wide range of reasons for choosing not to engage with your project, from lack of time and understanding to wilful sabotage.
- Engaging resistant stakeholders can be time-consuming but is ultimately worth it. There are a range of different approaches to try when it comes to engaging resisters.
- Plan enough time for engagement throughout the project, so you have provision in your schedule for doing the work of engagement. Don't assume you can fit a bit of engagement into your day – it doesn't work like that.

6

Conflict resolution

This chapter looks at what causes conflict on projects and how you can spot it. It also covers techniques for addressing conflict in your project environment including a basic process for starting to talk to others in conflict situations.

The language of conflict often talks about 'managing' conflict or 'resolving' conflict. In this chapter I'll use both terms.

Managing conflict tends to result in an outcome where the conflict is addressed and prevented from being an ongoing issue. However, someone typically loses out.

Resolving conflict tends to result in a positive outcome for both parties. This is where you can enable a win-win solution that addresses the cause of conflict and leaves both sides feeling positive about the result.

Ultimately, managers strive for conflict resolution because it presents the opportunity to add value and build positive relationships. Going for the win-win situation helps get away from the feeling that conflict is bad and always adds unnecessary struggle into your day.

On that positive note, let's define the term 'conflict'.

What is conflict?

The *APM Body of Knowledge* defines conflict like this:

> *Conflict arises when there are differing opinions and/or opposing interests between stakeholders that matter to the people involved and are not easily reconciled.*

Conflict is often considered a negative thing, and for good reason. Differing opinions and opposing interests can soon derail your project. You might start to spot factions. Arguments arise about who should be doing what, or who hasn't completed their work. The office becomes a highly charged environment, rife with tension between colleagues.

However, conflict isn't all bad. It's also the debate about how to build a software feature that prompts two engineers to rethink the original design and create something better. It's the trust and team building that come from an hour-long debate about something that won't matter in six months. It's the buy in that results from feeling as if you had your chance to put your points across.

While conflict at work is inevitable, your project will be put under unnecessary stress if you don't take active steps to address it. Conflict takes its toll on individuals too and unresolved tension is a fast way to lose your best people. If your team don't see you actively working on their behalf to address conflict and get everyone back to work, then that can have a knock-on impact on their respect for you as a leader.

There are huge project risks associated with not adequately addressing conflict. The practical steps for managing a conflict scenario are covered later in this chapter, but first let's look at the common causes of conflict on projects.

What causes conflict on projects?

In a project environment, there are so many potential causes of conflict. Projects deliver something new and people have differing opinions about what that should be and how it should be achieved.

The discussion to resolve the difference could be highly positive and productive, or it could result in a negative situation, which is what is typically thought of as 'conflict'.

Conflict can be associated with:

- the task being done;
- the process in use;
- the relationships between people on the team.

It can happen:

- within yourself (i.e. you reflecting on two positions and having conflicting feelings/opinions about how to proceed);
- between you and someone else;
- between two or more other people, with you caught up in their conflict;
- within the project team;

- between departments where there is a history or current flashpoint of organisational conflict.

As a project manager, you can also be the catalyst for conflict situations. Part of project management is to seek out what hasn't yet been done. You go looking for gaps. You chase people who haven't completed tasks, calling them out in team meetings for not being on track. You pick up mistakes because you start looking for them and because quality management is built into the way you run your projects.

Those actions can involve escalating problems – such as the underperforming colleague or a quality issue – to senior management. That puts you in direct conflict with the individual and perhaps the person you are escalating to, especially if the situation could be construed to make both of them look bad.

As a project manager, you oversee and direct work that is often done in a matrix structure. You're involved in the work of people who don't report to you. That can put you in conflict for their time because they are balancing the needs of their day job or other projects. And it can put you in a conflict situation with their line manager as well.

Conflict situations happen outside of work as well, but in your personal life you have more choice over whether to engage with the situation or step away from it.

While avoidance is a valid approach to dealing with conflict, as we'll see later in this chapter, for most professional situations, you are going to want to take some action and be seen to be taking action. Project, programme and portfolio success may depend on you taking active steps to resolve the situation.

Conflict is something you can't avoid as a project manager. But it isn't all bad. Conflict is a natural part of how people interact with each other and can be a positive force on a project.

While you shouldn't shy away from conflict, it does help to be prepared for it and this chapter will give you some strategies to do that.

At a conference[7], I asked delegates to comment on what caused conflict on their projects. The results are shown in Figure 6.1.

While that was quite a small and potentially unrepresentative sample of project delivery professionals, there were some interesting points raised.

---

[7] This was at a BCS, The Chartered Institute for IT, event in 2012.

Engaging stakeholders on projects

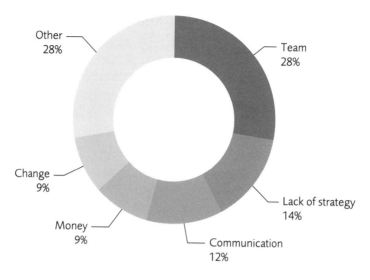

Figure 6.1 Causes of conflict on projects

Many types of conflict in teams have their roots in the relationships between team members. 'The team' accounts for over a quarter of all conflict causes. Some of the examples people gave included:

- lack of clarity about roles;
- personality clashes;
- ego;
- lack of respect;
- blame.

Take those out and you've hugely reduced the likelihood of conflict on your project team.

Lack of strategic direction and leadership was another flashpoint, with 14 per cent of delegates asked reporting that was a cause of conflict on their projects. Miscommunication and misunderstandings in the team came in at 12 per cent, followed by budget issues and people's not-so-positive responses to change both receiving nine per cent of the responses.

The 'Other' segment represents nearly 30 per cent of responses and here there were a multitude of themes including:

- aggressive timescales;
- lack of benefits;
- lack of knowledge;
- no project management method or structure to underpin success;
- confused requirements;
- the customer's expectations.

Easy win: Roles and responsibilities

A common cause of conflict on project teams is unclear roles and responsibilities. Perhaps someone feels a project task is not within the remit of their job. Lack of clarity about who is doing what can also result in two people working on the same tasks, causing resentment, as well as it being a waste of everyone's time.

Create a Roles and Responsibilities statement for your project that outlines who is responsible for what. Make sure everyone is comfortable with the document. It's a good way of identifying areas where responsibilities risk overlapping or where there are gaps and no one is taking ownership.

Identifying conflict on projects

Now it's clear that conflict is likely to happen on your project, how do you spot it?

The first step is to acknowledge that it could be happening. Dealing with conflict can feel awkward and out of our comfort zone. It's tempting to try to forget about the situation and assume it will resolve itself in time as that saves us the effort of having to take any special steps, especially if your default and preferred approach to conflict resolution is avoidance (I can speak from experience here).

However, ignoring conflict is rarely an appropriate response at work. It's time to look for conflict and step up to the challenge of facing it.

You will be more open to noticing and taking action about conflict if you first acknowledge that conflict is a possibility – even if acknowledging that means accepting you'll go out of your comfort zone to deal with it.

Let's look at some typical flashpoints for conflict on projects, so you can be watchful of these situations in your own work.

Engaging stakeholders on projects

The situations outlined below are purely illustrative and are not, of course, the only times you could be facing a conflict scenario at work. However, when you know the kind of things that drive those difficult situations, you can be better prepared for the challenges when they come.

Conflict during project kick off

You're at the start of the project while the team is working out exactly what is going to happen. This could be during the proposal stage, or business case preparation, or during the project kick off and initiation work.
There's a risk of conflict between the following groups:

- The client/sponsor and users:
  - about requirements or cost;
  - around agreeing the problem and the solution.
- other stakeholders:
  - Around differing project goals, expectations and priorities.
- The client/sponsor and the project manager:
  - around the requirements and how to get there.
- The client/sponsor and portfolio management.
  - about business case approval.

Conflict during project planning

Whether you're scoping your project fully at the outset, or using a hybrid or iterative approach and including regular planning sessions in your work, this is a time ripe with the potential for conflict.
There's a chance that you will see conflict between the following groups:

- The project manager and team leaders:
  - due to a difference of opinion about planning;
  - around roles and responsibilities;
  - around assigning risk ownership to people who don't believe they are accountable for it.
- The project manager and client/sponsor:
  - because once the detailed planning is done there may be a need to review scope to hit constraints like budget or deadlines.
- The project manager and suppliers:
  - around commercial agreements.

Conflict during project delivery

The work is underway. The team is busy completing tasks. On a project, this is where the bulk of the activity takes place. It's here that you will see the most possibility for conflict. Watch out for sparks between the following groups:

- The project manager and client/sponsor:
    - due to changes to scope and at any key decision-making points, for example, risk response plans.
- The project manager and team:
    - around resource or task allocation;
    - around what's realistic in the allocated time;
    - around how to approach the task.
- The project manager and team leaders:
    - around resource or task allocation;
    - around what's realistic in the allocated time;
    - around how to approach the task.
- The project manager and functional managers:
    - around resource or task allocation;
    - around what's realistic in the allocated time;
    - around how to approach the task (see a pattern?).
- The project manager and users:
    - as a result of quality control, testing and checking.

Deal with team conflict quickly during this time, because your project schedule can start to unravel if you let a situation stay unresolved for too long.

Conflict during project close

You've made it to the end of the project and now you're handing over to business as usual teams and closing the project down. What could go wrong here? You are at risk of project team conflict between the following groups:

- The project manager and the users or client/sponsor:
    - at the point of handover of deliverables if they are not what was expected.
- The project manager and the operational team:
    - as they might not want to receive the handover or take responsibility, or be ready for it.

Look out for potential conflict situations at this point in the project so you can tidy up any lingering awkward situations before you walk away from a project. You don't want to leave anyone with a sense that something is unfinished and it will be better for you too, knowing that you've done the best job you can to sort out the loose ends.

How to deal with conflicting priorities
Conflicting priorities happen when:

- You, or other stakeholders, are juggling multiple demands on your time;
- Your stakeholders have differing expectations of what the project will deliver for them.

While this situation might not be a problem for you at the moment, it is a conflict waiting to happen. It's best to address the issue of conflicting stakeholder expectations as early as you can.

Focus on where there is no consensus.

What are the points of conflict? Is it conflicting requirements within the project? Misaligned expectations? Expectations or concerns mapping (see Chapter 3) may have highlighted the lack of consensus. Is the schedule under pressure because there are too many tasks or projects happening at the same time and a lack of clarity around priorities?

Next, think about how you see the priorities. As a project professional, you can use your judgement to assess the situation. Given your understanding of the project's goals, which stakeholder's expectations align most closely to that? Given your understanding of the task priorities, which should be allocated more time?

Finally, think about who will validate those priorities and support your view. If it's an issue within your remit to resolve, talk to the individuals involved. If you need to escalate the problem, talk to your sponsor, project board, or your manager. They will either validate how you see the priorities, or reject them (in which case, ask them to offer guidance on what they see as the right approach).

Then you can take action on those priorities, for example, overruling a stakeholder who will not get what they want from the project, or delaying a low priority task to allow more time for critical work.

You may still have unhappy stakeholders at the end of this: someone hasn't got the outcome they wanted because their work hasn't been given priority. However, at least you have a way forward and support from the senior leadership team for this approach.

In many situations, the way through a conflict is simply sitting down with a colleague and facilitating a discussion, letting parties with differing opinions have their chance to speak and be heard.

In other situations, you'll recognise a major risk to the project as a result of this problem. You will need to actively lead the conflict to a satisfactory conclusion.

The Thomas-Kilmann conflict mode instrument is a structured way to approach conflict management.

The Thomas-Kilmann conflict mode instrument

The Thomas-Kilmann conflict mode instrument[8] (TKI) is a common model for considering approaches to dealing with conflict.

Originally development by Dr Kenneth W. Thomas and Dr Ralph H. Kilmann in 1974, it's a questionnaire that asks you to identify how you naturally react when faced with the opinions or concerns of two people (or groups) that don't align. It is a way of identifying your own natural reaction and response when you are in a conflict situation with someone.

Using a conflict model helps construct and shape your own experience of working with conflict management and resolution because:

1. You get a vocabulary that helps you define your default style when facing conflict, but also helps you understand what the other options are.
2. The basic principles can be understood easily and applied to your project at any time.

The conflict model outlined in Figure 6.2 is a useful tool for understanding a range of options available to you once you've identified a conflict situation. You have to deal with it and TKI gives you a selection of ways to do so.

[8] https://kilmanndiagnostics.com/overview-thomas-kilmann-conflict-mode-instrument-tki/

Engaging stakeholders on projects

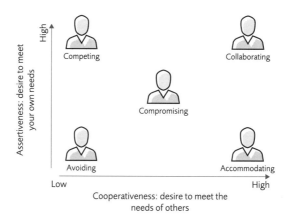

Figure 6.2 A common model for considering approaches to dealing with conflict

Source: Adapted from the Thomas Kilmann Conflict Mode Instrument.[9]

The conflict model looks at two different dimensions of your approach to conflict.

- Assertiveness: How far do you take your own concerns at the expense of others'? How strong is your desire to achieve your own objectives?
- Cooperativeness: How far do you go to satisfy the other person's concerns? How strong is your desire to help others achieve their objectives?

The model created by Thomas and Kilmann forces you to think about how far you will go to win and how much it matters to you that other people may have concerns that need to be met.

There are five different modes for responding to conflict, formed where the dimensions of assertiveness and cooperativeness align.

The conflict response modes are:

- avoiding;
- accommodating;
- competing;
- collaborating; and
- compromising.

[9] Figure 6.2 based on Dr Ralph Kilmann's version of the TKI Conflict Model, https://kilmanndiagnostics. com/overview-thomas-kilmann-conflict-mode-instrument-tki, copyright © 2009–2020 by Kilmann Diagnostics. All rights reserved. Accessed 28 February 2020.

The avoiding conflict mode

Avoiding is where you don't engage in conflict at all. It's an unassertive approach, because you aren't discussing or actively doing anything, and uncooperative, because you aren't helping the other person either. It's the 'do nothing' approach.

It might sound like it would never work but it can be effective if you use it in moderation and in the right situations.

Example: Two colleagues are arguing loudly. Their noise is disturbing other people in the open plan office. You talk to them calmly and tell them that when they've both calmed down you can help them work out some next steps. You suggest that one of them cools off in the meeting room and the other goes to the staff kitchen area.

What's happened here is that you haven't fixed the conflict. The team members still have something they need to resolve. You don't know the details yet and you will need to find out. You still need to address the underlying issue. If you don't do something, it's possible the problem gets worse over time.

Depending on the scenario, strategies you can use that fit into the Avoiding mode include:

- postponing the conversation until there is a better time to have it;
- picking your battles: avoid engaging in this conflict because you know there's another heated debate coming and it serves your purpose more to engage in that one;
- using diplomacy to avoid discussing a potential source of conflict at this time;
- moving away from a threatening situation.

The accommodating conflict mode

Accommodating is what happens when you are directed to do something. For example, if your project sponsor directs you to take a certain course of action to handling a risk.

It's an unassertive response but it shows high cooperation because your personal preferences are overlooked and overridden. You accommodate the action, preference or outcome put forward by the other party.

You might think that if you end up in this situation, you've "lost" but sometimes it isn't worth winning.

Engaging stakeholders on projects

Example: A project team member checks their annual leave requests with you and you notice that a key task they are scheduled to do clashes with their time off. You're unhappy about them taking the time off and they explain that they have already agreed a colleague will take over the work. It's not worth arguing this point as the work will still get done, so you agree to their leave request.

Strategies that fit into the Accommodating mode include:

- being generous in accepting the proposal put forward by the other party, or doing so out of charity;
- obeying an order or rule even if you feel you don't need to;
- yielding to someone else's point of view because they are in a position of authority.

Be careful how often you use this strategy personally. If you capitulate too often, people might start to see you as a walkover.

> **Closing the corridor**
> A project manager was based in a hospital for a short period during a project deployment. There was a corridor through the cancer ward that provided a shortcut to the rest of the building. However, the noise of people walking through the ward was disruptive to patients undergoing chemotheraphy treatment, and this had been reported on patient feedback surveys. The hospital management team decided to close off the corridor to staff who were using it as a shortcut.
>
> The longer route was inconvenient for the project manager and her team trying to access different areas of the hospital as part of their work. However, they respected the corridor closure, *even when there were no patients on the ward*, because it was the rule.

The competing conflict mode

Competing is also called 'Forcing'.

This method of responding to conflict is high up on the assertive scale and it's uncooperative, just as the name suggests.

This is where you force the other person to take on your solution. You are defending your position while they "lose".

You can only really take this approach when you have some kind of legitimate power that specifically relates to the situation you're in. Examples of legitimate power include:

- you are more senior than the other person in the management hierarchy;
- you have control of something relevant to the situation, like the budget or resources;
- you have expertise relevant to the situation that the other person doesn't have.

You could also exert authority in this kind of situation simply because you are better at arguing than they are.

Example: You're working on a building site and a colleague says they don't want to wear the health and safety personal protective equipment. In this situation, you have to force the team member to comply with the regulations.

Conflict resolution strategies you can use in these situations include:

- telling someone else what to do;
- referring people to a policy or regulation that dictates what must be done;
- issuing a written directive that tells someone else what to do.

However, you might not feel that you have 'resolved' conflict if you use these strategies. You've managed the situation, made a decision and moved a project on, but you've probably ruffled some feathers at the same time. Forcing is something to use only when you really have to.

Policies: The unsung conflict management strategy

Organisational and team policies are a way to defuse conflict relatively easily. It's hard to argue with an agreed and documented governing framework on how work is done. Plus, if someone does choose to create conflict around a point covered by a policy, you have that documentation to fall back on. It's not you personally disagreeing with the individual, it's a corporate policy that everyone must abide by.

Policies can be used to address issues with behaviour, ethics, attendance, timekeeping, dress code, expense management and more. Within the project environment, there may be PMO policies on the way certain project practices should be carried out.

Give a copy of any relevant policies to new starters on the team so they are aware of the standards they need to adhere to.

The compromising conflict mode

Compromising is moderately assertive and moderately cooperative. It's a halfway position and it's very commonly used. It can also be a quick way to get through a conflict, if you can rapidly settle on a compromise that is mutually acceptable.

When you compromise, you don't get exactly what you want. However, neither does the other party. Instead, you come to an amicable solution you can both agree on. It's a helpful option where you find yourself with an impasse: it's impossible for both stakeholders to get exactly what they want and you don't have time to facilitate long, heated debates that might not get a resolution anyway.

Example: The team say the sprint should be two weeks long but you want it to be four weeks. You compromise and agree that sprints will be three weeks.

Conflict resolution strategies you can use in this mode include:

- discussion;
- splitting the difference and meeting in the middle e.g. with fees or timescales;
- exchanging concessions: you both give something up.

The collaborating conflict mode

Collaborating is an assertive way of resolving problems. It's also very cooperative.

Neither party tries to avoid the conflict and neither approaches discussions with a view to "win". Instead, you work together to look into the problems and come up with solutions where you both get what you want.

This can be time-consuming because you need to invest enough time in understanding the underlying expectations and desires from each party so they can be adequately met by the new solution.

As a facilitator, you'll need to assertively stand up for what is in the project's best interests while aligning goals with the other party to achieve the win-win outcome you both want.

Strategies to try here include:

- discussion and active listening;
- brainstorming;
- facilitation;
- creative problem solving.

Collaborating can sound like the "best" way to manage conflict, but the "best" way can be any of the conflict management approaches, depending on the situation. If my young son runs towards the edge of a busy road and is at risk of putting himself in danger, I'm not going to spend time collaborating. All the conflict resolution strategies can be useful in the right situation.

As you've read through the different modes to address conflict, has one jumped off the page for you as a description of what you would normally seek to do?

For example, you may love the buzz of negotiating a compromise, so find yourself naturally relying on that approach to resolve conflict more than the other options. Or your role as a senior leader in the organisation means everyone looks to you for guidance and you tend to use the competing mode because it's fast and expected of you. That may work much of the time, but may not be appropriate for other types of conflict.

You may already have a feel for your personal preference for handling conflict. If not, there is information in the Action Steps section at the end of this chapter which will help you identify your conflict resolution preferences.

The TKI instrument provides a framework for understanding different approaches to managing conflict. People do typically have a natural inclination towards a particular approach. However, you are capable of using all the different modes. The challenge is to select an approach that is going to be appropriate to each situation.

Take each conflict on merit and use the conflict model in Figure 6.2 to assess what would be the best approach to use in that scenario. If your first approach isn't successful, you can always try a different tactic.

Remember, different approaches take different lengths of time and require different energy levels. It may not be necessary to invest in achieving your own and someone else's objectives at the same time. Think about how much the conflict matters to the project's overall objectives and how important it is to maintain a good working relationship with this stakeholder for the rest of the project. You may choose a different strategy for conflict management at the start of a project than at the end, for example, where your relationship with the stakeholder is coming to a close.

Conflict is an inevitable part of working on projects, programmes and at portfolio level. It's not something to worry about. Arm yourself with a few techniques for dealing with difficult situations before they happen, because that can give you the confidence to tackle conflict as it arises. Then everyone can get back to work.

Understand your role in conflict situations

As we have seen, conflict happens at work. But it's not always your battle to fight.

Think about who is going to feel let down if you step in and are seen to be taking sides. Often, managers and leaders on project teams – and more broadly in the workplace – need to be seen as being neutral.

Understanding the boundaries of your role as a project manager can help you get the team to a resolution. In other words: it's not always your job to resolve conflict.

You can facilitate the conflict resolution, but unless you are one of the parties "in" the conflict – for example, if there is conflict between you and a line manager – then it's not your role to find the solution.

They own the disagreement. You own the facilitation of the resolution.

You also have another role to play: that of ensuring the project team stay engaged in a positive sense to minimise the risk of unhealthy conflict.

The more the team know, like and trust each other, the more likely it is that conflict can be handled in a constructive way. As a project leader, think about how you can create opportunities for the team to discuss differences in a positive way.

Here are some examples:

- Create an environment where open, honest, respectful conversation is the norm.
- Make the team goals clear and create buy-in for those goals by aligning them to the reward structure where appropriate, to minimise the risk of individual agendas taking priority.
- Recognise and thank people who do speak up with differing views.
- Foster inclusivity and welcome diverse opinions because they make the project deliverables stronger.
- Highlight areas where there is agreement as a foundation for discussing areas where there is not.
- Create the expectation of cabinet responsibility. This means that if your view isn't the 'winning' view, you get onboard with the decision taken and deliver what's required with good grace.
- Provide training on interpersonal skills and problem solving and even conflict resolution.

A basic process for managing conflict

You know that conflict is likely to occur at work and you're primed to spot it. You understand what your responses could be, but what does using that response actually look like in practice?

A basic process for planning to address a conflict is described in Figure 6.3.

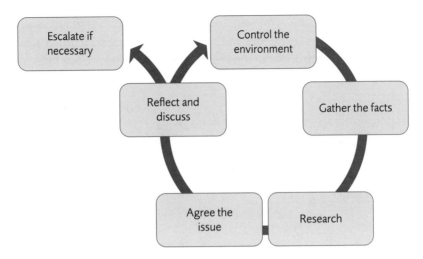

Figure 6.3 A basic process for addressing conflict

Spending even a little bit of time thinking through how best to address the problem can give you the confidence to tackle conflict in a positive way. Here's how the planning process breaks down.

1. Pick the location and environment

If you need to address a colleague's poor performance, your team meeting is not the place to do it. The first part of your preparation for addressing conflict is to think about the environment and how you can control or influence it to get the best possible outcome.

Find a time when neither of you have to rush off to another meeting shortly after. Book a private meeting room out of earshot from the rest of the team, or go off-site.

If you are discussing an issue with a supplier, it might be prudent to hold the meeting on neutral ground, like at an external meeting venue. Or you may decide that you want the 'home advantage' of meeting at your office location.

Your choice of environment matters. Think about where this conversation is going to happen and plan to make it as advantageous for you both as possible.

2. Gather the facts

Let's say you're helping two colleagues resolve their differences over how a piece of work was done. Gather the facts. Meet them both individually to hear their side of the story.

Dig into the data. Ideally, you want to get as far away from emotion as you can, while acknowledging that people will naturally feel emotional about situations that are out of their control or that they feel passionately about. Look for evidence, so you are going into the debate as prepared as you can be.

> Once, I was part of a discussion where two colleagues were arguing. As we worked through the conversations, we found that they both actually agreed and were arguing for the same point. Their communication styles were at such odds with each other that neither had understood what their colleague was truly advocating for.

3. Research and recognise stakeholder power and personal views

Next, you need to find out about the people who are in the conflict, whether that is someone with an opposing view to you, or two colleagues or groups whom you are supporting to reconcile their differences.

In particular, consider the formal and informal power structures in the organisation and where the individuals fit. That can help you see what kind of conflict mode they might choose to manage the problem.

Find out what they believe the issue to be and how they wish it to be resolved. Ask the question, "What would be a good outcome for you?" or "How would you like to see this resolved?"

It could also be useful to discuss the problem with people outside of those immediately involved in the conflict to provide insight into the motivating factors that are driving the conflict.

Note: The conflict may have been caused by underlying factors unrelated to the issue, for example something going on at home, workplace stress etc. People may not want to share the specifics with you, or even tell you that anything might be affecting their behaviour. Simply be conscious of the fact that there might be something else influencing their behaviour that you are not aware of.

4. Meet and agree on the issue

Get the conflicting parties together, at the time and location you've chosen. Agree what the issue is. Speak plainly: "I've asked to meet with you today because I know there is a conflict between what the Marketing department thinks the project is going to deliver and what the IT department believe is feasible in the timescales. It's important we talk about the issues on both sides so the project can continue to move forward. Is that what you think too?"

Another example:

> "I was looking at the timesheets and I noticed Anthony has been putting in a lot of overtime. When I looked into it, I realised he has been doing a lot of work that we could share out between other team members and in fact, some of you might be better placed to do the tasks than Anthony. Plus, the project doesn't have a big budget for overtime, so if we continue this pattern we're going to have issues with finance. Shall we look at what we've got coming up in the next month so we can make sure the work is distributed evenly?"

A statement like the one above is a gentle introduction to a debate about defining roles and responsibilities, time management, everyone taking responsibility for their own workloads and for gaining agreement that there is a project issue worth resolving.

The aim is to describe the problem in neutral language, using facts, and gain agreement on what the issue really is.

Conflict and blame

When you articulate the issue causing the conflict, do so in a way that does not apportion blame. It's not helpful to say, "Claire messed up the solution design so we've spent the last three weeks building something no one wants. And because no one cares about quality on this team, no one thought to say anything!" – even if you secretly believe that to be true.

Blame makes people defensive and that slows you down from getting to a resolution.

If something has gone wrong, and you feel the discussion is about to move into the blame game, proactively take the blame yourself. I've used this technique many times and it's always effective. It takes the pressure off your project team colleagues. As the project leader, it makes sense that the buck stops with you. It's a way to defuse the situation and it often leads to someone else in the room voluntarily talking about how they contributed to the problem as well.

5. Reflect and discuss

During this step, you hopefully come to a conclusion that allows the project to move on, even if it means someone has accepted a concession or had their views overruled.

You may not be able to conclude the discussions in one meeting, and that's OK. Each individual may want to reflect and discuss options with their own teams, before meeting again.

If you are going to carry on the conversation another time, make sure that a date and time is booked before you conclude your first meeting. This mitigates the risk that you won't have time to resolve the conflict properly.

Note: Don't make promises you can't keep. If you need to get approval from your manager or team before agreeing to a resolution, say that.

6. Escalate if necessary

Finally, it's worth noting that in a project, programme or even a portfolio role, you may not be able to resolve all types of conflict all the time. You may need to escalate an issue, or ask someone else to arbitrate on the problem where it cannot be resolved by the parties involved.

Know your escalation route so you can raise the problem with people who can help you (and your colleagues) move past the issue.

Escalation routes could be:

- project, programme or portfolio governance roles e.g. the project sponsor;
- a neutral mediator from inside the organisation (make sure the individual is agreed on by both sides);
- an external mediator (again, agreed on by both sides);
- an arbitration service e.g. where you wish to avoid conflict escalating into litigation or industrial action.

Formal contracts with suppliers or clients will include escalation routes and plans for arbitration but you may not find the same level of documentation for how to escalate an internal issue.

It is worth creating a governance protocol that lays out how project conflicts will be resolved. Consider what roles at programme and portfolio level form part of the escalation chain. Having something documented at the beginning of the project, or as part of the core PMO processes, will help you if you ever need to use a formal approach to escalating an issue.

Those six steps form a basic process for addressing conflict. On top of all that you need to have top notch ethics, empathy, remain objective and be sensitive to the needs of all the people involved while striving for the best solution. It's not easy, but it is something that you can practice. And it does get easier the more you do it.

What to do when you can't plan your conflict-handling approach

Sometimes you won't have time to plan how to deal with conflict, or you'll be put on the spot. All the conflict modes you could choose will fly out of your mind. In those situations, feel free to say, "I need to gather some more information/consult my team/reflect on that and get back to you." Try not to get drawn into conflict if you aren't ready to discuss it right now.

A fast apology is another way of stopping an argument mid-flow. It might not be appropriate (or work) all the time, but it is hard to maintain an argument with someone who is saying sorry or agreeing with you.

See the box for some other useful phrases for defusing conflict at work.

Phrases for defusing conflict at work

- I'm sorry that happened.
- I'm sorry you feel like that.
- You're right, we definitely should have . . . to avoid this.
- What I hear you saying is . . .
- I can see there's a problem. I'm looking into it now.
- What do you need from me right now?
- That's my fault. The buck stops with me.
- Tell me more about this and how it's affecting you.
- What can I do next time to make this situation easier for you?
- I think I understand where you are coming from, but I have a different view.
- How can I help?
- What's your biggest concern about this?
- Shall we take a break, think this over and reconvene later?
- I'm hearing you say one thing, but I'm seeing you do something else. What's causing that?

- What can we do to make sure this doesn't happen again?
- I don't know, but I'll find out.
- I know someone who has the answer to this. I'll get back to you in 15 minutes.
- Is this the right time for you to talk about this?
- What if . . .?
- It doesn't feel to me like we need to agree on this because . . . What do you think?

If you are forced into a conflict discussion where you aren't ready for it, do the best you can and don't worry about how you 'performed'. Remember, it's only work. The conflicts managers get involved with on projects rarely have life-altering consequences. There is likely to be another time for you to put your point of view.

It can be emotionally and physically draining when your workplace feels highly charged and there are many conflicts to navigate each day. It's important to remain personally resilient in times of conflict at work as that will help you maintain perspective and keep leading the team. There are tips for building resilience in Chapter 7.

One issue, two conflicts

A software programme manager was approached by the company's head of finance.

Conflict 1: Changing resources.
The head of finance wasn't happy with the performance of the project manager assigned to lead the finance project within her programme. He asked for that project manager to be removed.

The programme manager didn't have an alternative project manager available, but she had to accommodate the head of finance's request, as he had more hierarchical power than she did and his support was critical for the programme's success.

Conflict 2: Telling the project manager.
The programme manager knew she had to remove the project manager from the project.

She picked the location, deciding to take him out for coffee.

She gathered the facts, understanding why the project manager had not made a good impression on the Finance team, despite being a technically competent and reliable project manager with a good reputation elsewhere in the business.

She thought about how he was going to feel about being switched into another role and recognised the head of finance's power and views in this situation.

She met the project manager for coffee. They discussed the points raised by the head of finance and what that meant for the finance project. He agreed that there was a culture or personality clash. He knew he wasn't having the impact he had hoped to make and that affecting change was difficult.

They reflected on how they could make the switch of project managers easier both on him and whoever was brought in as a replacement, coming up with a knowledge transfer plan.

Handling conflict in virtual teams

Conflict in virtual teams can be harder to spot and resolve because of the environment you are operating in. It is a lot harder to notice conflict when you can't read the body language.

However, it's easy to spot conflict in written electronic communications. Most people have met a colleague who is prepared to be abrupt and sometimes downright rude in email in a way that you know they wouldn't be face-to-face.

Many of the approaches for managing and resolving conflict that have already been discussed in this chapter will be applicable for virtual teams. Here are a few extra points to consider.

Lead by example. Don't make snide comments about your colleagues. People listen – even people who you might not think would be listening. Make a point of always being respectful, inclusive and professional, even with colleagues who know you well and whom you consider to be friends.

Create opportunities to talk. Have regular team meetings. While I don't advocate having meetings when there isn't any need to, you can always cancel a regular check in if you don't need it, or spend five minutes on a call allowing people to air any issues they've met this week.

Ask what issues are out there and what people need help with.

Spend one-to-one time with team members as well, so they have an opportunity to raise concerns with you outside of the team setting.

Limit the amount of emails you send. Phil Simon writes, in *Message Not Received*, "After three emails, someone needs to pick up the phone. Refuse to engage in email conversations." If a three-email rule seems a bit tight to you, pick a number. Five is good. If an email chain goes beyond three (or five) messages, take it off email. You need to talk. Make that a team rule.

Create a level playing field for meetings. If some of you are in the same location and some are not, have everyone dial in so the meeting experience is equitable.

Be alert to the prospect that virtual teams can struggle with conflict and watch out for anything that looks, sounds or feels out of the ordinary so you can deal with it quickly.

Handling conflict in meetings

There are two types of low-level conflict that you will see commonly in meetings: detours and rudeness.

Dealing with detours

A detour is a topic that comes up in the meeting that isn't on the agenda. Perhaps it's an issue that arose since the agenda was prepared, or perhaps someone is trying to use meeting time to discuss a topic not aligned to the meeting's objectives. Either way, detours create tension between the meeting chair and the person trying to raise the topic.

As meeting chair, you have the discretion to go with detours or to shut them down. Go with it if you have the time, the participants seem interested and you feel it's a valid conversation to be having.

If it is too off-topic, politely suggest that the discussion is "taken off line" which means the relevant people will carry on the conversation at a different time. You can also use a flipchart on the wall as a 'parking lot' to note down off-topic discussions so they remain in full sight of everyone.

The phrasing for shutting down a detour could look like this:

"That's a great suggestion, but we don't have enough time to go into it in as much detail as it deserves right now. Let's add it to the parking lot and if we have time at the end we can go back to it. For now, shall we carry on with the plans for Quarter 4?"

If you decide to shut down the detour, remember to note that the conversation still needs to happen. Include it as a meeting action, allocated to the people who have to continue their conversation. If necessary, add the topic to the agenda next time so they can summarise their discussion for the group.

Dealing with rudeness and unprofessional behaviour

People look to you as chair to set the tone for the meeting. Make sure you give everyone a turn to speak and manage the flow of the conversation so that all voices are heard, not just the loudest ones. Feel free to interrupt a verbose colleague and ask them to get to the point.

Encourage the group to listen to each other and not speak over each other; step in if that happens. Ask questions, especially if you notice other people in the room who look like they don't understand.

You should also step in if the discussion stoops to unprofessional language or comments. A quick, "Let's keep it about performance, not personalities," should help reinforce expectations of language and behaviour. You may choose to follow up with the individual who made unprofessional remarks after the meeting if you feel it is appropriate to do so.

If you feel the conversation is becoming heated between a couple of people, ask a quieter colleague a direct question. That can help lower the intensity of the debate and redirect attention in the room.

A note on virtual meetings: as people tend to multi-task or pay less attention when they're on a conference call or web meeting than meeting in person, conflict may be harder to spot. As people are typically less engaged, they may choose to contribute less to the meeting instead of raise an issue head on. Listen out for changes in the contribution patterns of your regular attendees. Who has stopped participating? Who is talking up more? This could be a sign that something is going on with the participants and warrants a one-to-one chat with the people concerned to see if they have anything they'd like to raise with you in person.

Action steps

- Think about a situation where you have compromised in the past. With hindsight, was there a way to create a win-win scenario instead?
- Talk to your HR team to find out if they have access to the formal TKI assessment. Can you take it with your team and compare your results?
- Reflect on the latest conversations within your virtual team. Could there be any conflict lurking that you've been overlooking? It's time to confront it.

Key takeaways

- Conflict management for project managers is part of the daily engagement with stakeholders and the team.
- Conflict can happen at any point in the project.
- It can happen for numerous reasons, often to do with misunderstandings and misaligned expectations.
- There are many ways to resolve conflict at work. Try a few of the techniques mentioned in this chapter and arm yourself with some strategies that feel comfortable for you.
- Deal with conflict as soon as you can to stop it becoming a larger problem.

7

Skills builder

This chapter provides a deeper dive into 10 of the interpersonal skills and behaviours that are beneficial for successful stakeholder engagement. There are also tips for improving your practice and developing your skills in these areas.

This book has already talked extensively about communication and conflict resolution, so those skills – which would normally make my top 10 – have been set aside for now. There are so many interpersonal and technical skills that are useful when engaging others that it has been necessary to streamline and prioritise what can be covered in this section.

Whole books have been written about these topics. Selected further reading is listed in the Bibliography at the end of the book. The goal in the next few pages is to provide an overview and some quick action steps for boosting your abilities (or confirming your existing level of abilities), thus making it easier to do the work of engaging others.

The skills covered in this chapter are listed below.

1. Negotiation.
2. Influencing.
3. Listening.
4. Business acumen.
5. Resilience.
6. Credibility.
7. Assertiveness.
8. Contextual awareness.
9. Cultural awareness.
10. Ethical awareness.

In practice, excellent project professionals do all of these things without thinking about them. The skills become a part of how work gets done. The portfolio manager in your company doesn't wake up and think, "Today I'm going to do some really good influencing." More often than not, the influencing just happens as part of the inherent, subtle, interactions with others during the day. Perhaps they are done consciously, perhaps not. The more you master the skills, the more they become an integral part of how you do your job and not a specific tool you take out to wield at a given moment.

Leadership is also a core skill, but it happens as a result of all the skills listed here, and others.

Before looking at the skills, it's worth taking a moment to consider how much time and energy you should put into professional development and building your competence across the domain.

How much effort should you put into building skills?

Project delivery professionals are lifelong learners. Over the course of a career, the best project professionals remain curious. They are constantly learning and developing new skills, staying up to date with tools and techniques that work to generate engagement and create an environment for successful delivery.

However, sometimes there is little value in bolstering an area you have identified as a personal weakness. For example, let's say negotiation is not, and has never been, your strong point. You could spend thousands of pounds on negotiation courses and resources. You could practice your skills regularly, putting in hours of preparation prior to a negotiation. And you still might only ever be average.

Is it worth pursuing this avenue, at the detriment of other skills you could be developing? Or could you fill your personal gap with someone on the team who is an excellent negotiator? The time you spend on trying to improve your negotiating could be better spent on something else.

Sometimes there's a sensible trade-off to be had. The more you can use expertise on the team so that everyone is playing to their strengths and operating at their best level, the more successful the team will be and the more time you will have to do your best work.

It's obviously good in theory to build your skills in a range of different areas. But be realistic about your personal capabilities and the level you can achieve with a reasonable amount of time and effort. A better 'win' for the team and the organisation overall could be for you to work alongside a colleague who has complementary skills to your own.

With that in mind, let's dive into the skills that are fundamental to being able to create successful stakeholder relationships.

Contextual awareness

Contextual awareness is the ability to select the appropriate time, place and individuals for a particular interaction.

For example, you wouldn't talk to a colleague about their poor performance in front of the whole team, or in an open plan office. You wouldn't tell the project sponsor that their idea won't work in a project board meeting in front of their peers.

Contextual awareness can be gained from taking a systems thinking approach or carrying out business process modelling to understand the environment in which you are operating. It's also the product of being able to read a situation and make the best possible choices at the time.

Tips for improving practice

- Ask yourself before each stakeholder engagement: "How can I create the context for success?"
- Think about how you can research the organisational context and find out more about the operating environment before planning to engage.

Cultural awareness

Cultural awareness relates to the background and values of both the organisation and the people involved.

Organisational culture refers to how things get done in the organisation. It is the set of (sometimes unwritten) rules that dictate and influence how individuals and teams behave.

Large projects and programmes often create sub-cultures within the organisational culture, especially when the team is made up of individuals from a variety of entities. A common project culture can bring the team together under one common set of goals and values.

Your stakeholder analysis work will reveal clues about the cultural identifiers typically associated with the culture or sub-culture an individual is from. This kind of desk-based analysis and assumption is no substitute for getting to know stakeholders as individuals.

It's impossible to harness people power if you don't know the people as people.

Tips for improving practice

- Check you've understood the cultural norms of an organisation before making a decision or moving forward with an engagement scenario. Ask a trusted colleague, "Do you think that will work here?"
- Embrace diversity of all kinds on the project.
- Talk openly to the team and stakeholders about your culture and values to encourage dialogue.
- Don't make cultural assumptions. Be curious.

Influencing

The *APM Body of Knowledge* defines influencing as:

> *The act of affecting the behaviours and actions of others.*

There are many ways to achieve this including:

- convincing others with logic, data or stories;
- negotiating with others;
- inspiring others;
- involving others and recognising their contribution;
- coercing others.

It is difficult to influence others when you have no relationship with them. The first step in influencing should always be to build a relationship where you can with the individuals involved.

Much of stakeholder engagement falls under the category of influencing and needs to be considered with ethical implications in mind. Ann Pilkington writes about this in her paper, 'Communications shape reality' in the book *The Practitioner's Handbook of Project Performance*. She writes:

> *There is perhaps a conflict here between persuading stakeholders to a particular course of action versus engaging with stakeholders to enable them to influence the course of action. Having said that, there will be times when a project really needs people to work or act differently and will need to consider how comfortable it feels in adopting persuasion techniques.*

Ultimately, you need to make a judgement call about what you are influencing others to do and how that fits within the moral and ethical framework of the project.

Tips for improving practice

- It's easier to influence someone if the conditions are right. Consider the context, the individuals involved and how those individuals will react to each other and the setting.
- Reflect on whether your actions are likely to improve, worsen or create conflict. If so, how are you going to respond to that?
- Ask questions. Questions help you understand the position of the other person and thus allow you to tailor further discussion, communication methods or engagement activities to best address the need at the time.

Negotiation

Negotiation is a type of influencing that warrants a separate mention. Negotiation skills are crucial for project management. Whether discussing what services a vendor can offer you or talking to senior stakeholders to secure resources from their area, approaching negotiating professionally will give you better results. It is also a useful skill for conflict resolution.

A successful negotiation has three steps: planning, engagement and closure.

In the planning step, consider what the goals of the other party might be and what could be motivating them. Think about what you ideally want to get out of the negotiation and what you would settle for. Gain clarity on the level of authority you have to ask for or offer a concession to the other party.

Allow enough time to engage effectively. Negotiations turn out better for both parties when you are not rushed or under pressure from an outside source. Contracts often need to be reviewed by several people on both sides and potentially drafted and redrafted a few times. Plan enough time to complete the discussions.

When the negotiation is coming to a close, make sure there is clarity about the decision on both sides. Complete the necessary documentation and move on to implement what was agreed.

Tips for improving practice

- Notice when you are negotiating in everyday life. Think about what you could do differently next time.
- Consciously prepare for your next negotiation.
- Many people feel stressed or nervous during formal negotiations. Think about how negotiating makes you feel and consider ways to manage your emotions during the discussion.
- Practice active listening. Listen for what the other party wants and any issues that need to be addressed.

Listening

Active listening is where you listen – really listen – to what is being said.

Too often, people are preoccupied with their own agendas, skipping forward in their head to the part in the conversation where they get to talk again. Try not to do that. Instead be present in the moment.

A feature of active listening is that the listener provides feedback on what they are hearing. This gives you the opportunity to express empathy as well.

One way to show you are actively listening and to take in the information being shared is to reflect back the speaker's comments. Summarise and rephrase what they have said, using your own words. This shows them that you have understood the point they are making and gives them the opportunity to correct you if you haven't.

Tips for improving practice

- Listen with your whole body: watch the speaker's body language. Are they signaling with their body the same things they are saying out loud?
- Too much reflecting back can be annoying for the speaker, but a little bit shows you are paying attention. Use phrases like:
  - What I'm hearing is . . .
  - If I can just paraphrase to make sure I've understood . . .
  - Can I summarise that? These are the main points I've taken from what you've said so far . . .
  - Tell me if I've got this right . . .

- Reflect back emotion. Use phrases like:
  - That sounds like it is very frustrating for you.
  - I'm picking up that you were disappointed in the behaviour of the team.
  - You seem a bit [emotion].

  You'll need to judge the situation before you reflect back the emotion you've heard. Telling the CEO that their concern about a project delay "sounds like it must be very frustrating" could come across as patronising and inappropriate.

Business acumen

Business acumen is about being able to see the bigger commercial picture – the commercial reality of the world outside your project – and acting accordingly.

If you don't already know, find out how your company makes money. That might seem like a simple question but many businesses have multiple income streams and multiple customer groups. How are the needs of each of these groups prioritised?

Business acumen also relates to the operational context of your work, whether you're in a traditional business environment, start up, charity or any other sector.

Being able to see the bigger picture and industry context gives you 'acumen': the ability to make good decisions and to use your professional judgement wisely.

You don't have to have years of experience to have professional judgement. In most cases you simply need to apply common sense and good project management skills like involving the right stakeholders, reading the landscape, using your emotional intelligence and applying what you see to the recommendations you make.

Stakeholders are often most interested in project cost and the time it is going to take to finish the work. Your business acumen comes into play hugely here.

You should be able to talk about the business context and financial context of your project as it sits within the wider operational strategy.

You don't have to be a whizz at reading the profit and loss statement. Business acumen is far more about asking sensible questions, assimilating information and making connections. Think about the value your project delivers and how that aligns to what the business values. Think about strategic fit. All project decisions should be taken with consideration of the bigger commercial picture.

It makes you a better project manager than someone who simply works through the plan and doesn't look outside the walls of the project.

Tips for improving practice

- Source and read your company's annual report (if one is produced).
- Calculate the direct financial impact of your project on the company's products or services. Is it decreasing the margin on your offerings or increasing it?
- Establish how your project is going to affect customer service. If it doesn't, how could you address customer service through the work you are doing, either to maintain it or make service even better?
- Talk to the finance team about how best to manage your project budget. Don't sit on reserves of capital if you don't need them until later in the year. If you have large bills to pay, make sure they know in advance so cash flow isn't affected.
- Review your project schedule. Is there any value in being able to deliver faster? Perhaps you'd be able to realise some benefits more quickly, which, in the bigger scheme of things, would offset the cost of an additional resource required to do the work faster. Talk to your sponsor if you spot anything.

Resilience

Resilience is the ability to adapt and recover during and after periods of workplace stress or other adverse situations.

Projects naturally have periods where work is busy and the environment is highly charged. There may be many interpersonal conflicts to negotiate, along with tight deadlines and a difficult corporate political environment. All of this contributes to workplace stress. From time to time, individuals may be under excessive pressure at work.

Resilience is one way humans cope with pressurised situations, along with creating structures and a supportive environment to ensure stress at work is manageable.

Acknowledge that there are stressors in the environment for you and your team, even if you aren't feeling them yet. Be alert to sources of pressure and negative stress.

Talking about the likelihood of change can sometimes offset some of the pressure felt when change does happen. Encourage flexibility and show willingness to adapt.

Tips for improving practice

- Look out for your colleagues. Watch for signs of undue, negative stress. Encourage personal wellbeing in the team, for example, encouraging everyone to take a lunch break away from their desk and leading from the front by doing that yourself.
- Avoid negative people. Where possible, surround yourself with colleagues who lift each other up. Create a positive project culture and address underlying team conflict or negativity.
- Show progress towards project goals. Demonstrating what progress is being made is a way to highlight that despite the difficulties, the project is moving in the right direction.

Credibility

Credibility helps with stakeholder engagement because people are more prepared to work with and be influenced by someone who is a credible authority in the organisation already, even if you don't wield traditional power through the hierarchical structure.

Being credible helps you achieve engagement and influence in a positive way. Credibility is made up of two elements: competence and confidence.

Competence is essential. More importantly, people need to know you are competent. Assess yourself against a competence framework for project managers or ask for a 360 degree feedback assessment.

Your stakeholders won't have access to the same competence framework as you are using. Even if they do, it's unlikely they will mentally compare you to that. Instead, they will be looking to see if you approach your work professionally and deliver the results they are expecting.

Confidence is the second factor. You won't be considered influential if you struggle to speak up in meetings or hold the floor if challenged. People need to look at you and think that you know what you are talking about and that they can trust your recommendations. They won't feel that if you mumble and your body language implies you aren't sure of the answer.

You will feel more confident if you know your subject. Prepare before meetings. Know the key facts about project performance and be able to communicate them at short notice if you need to.

The way people interpret your credibility is predicated on what you do, what you say and how you say it.

Tips for improving practice

- Work on your technical project management skills. Identify areas where you feel you could improve and build on those. Use a competence framework to help.[10]
- Get a certification and when you pass exams, put your post-nominal letters in your email signature.
- Consider your body language and take a confident stance, whether you are physically visible to people or not. Confidence comes through in your voice on the phone as well!

For a long time, I didn't want to use my post-nominals to show my credentials to colleagues at work. In a healthcare setting, many of my colleagues were doctors, professors, or held senior nursing qualifications or other relevant industry professional certifications. My project management achievements didn't feel industry-relevant. Plus, I believed that my experience and track record spoke for itself. I didn't need to 'flaunt' my credentials in my email signature. It felt like showing off.

However, on one project I started working with a brand new group of stakeholders; people who had never interacted with me. People who had email signatures with long lists of all the posts, awards and credentials they held. It was a business change project with high strategic importance and a high degree of uncertainty. We shifted direction multiple times and to an outsider, it could easily have looked like we had no idea what we were doing despite there being a clear goal.

I felt it was time to give weight to the fact that we were an experienced team. I earned those post-nominals, so I was going to use them.

I have no evidence that putting letters after my name in my email signature made the slightest bit of difference to how I was perceived by stakeholders, but I finally felt that my professional achievements and experience were worth recognising.

It is not showing off to use the designations you have been granted by a professional body. It's a demonstrable way to show your expertise in the field. Don't wait as long as I did before showing your colleagues what you are capable of.

---

[10] For example, https://www.apm.org.uk/resources/find-a-resource/competence-framework/

Assertiveness

Assertiveness is about how to stand your ground under pressure while respecting the needs of other stakeholders. It's not – or it shouldn't be – about making sure you win at all costs.

Assertiveness is important for making sure the views of all relevant parties are heard. You can be assertive on behalf of a silent party by giving them the floor in a meeting or representing their views.

Take an assertive stance to protect the processes that keep your project functioning effectively, such as requiring all changes to go through a thorough analysis.

Assertiveness is a double-edged sword in collaborative, people-centered teams. Too much and you risk appearing as closed to engagement or discussion, or at worst, bullying. Too little and it's difficult to keep control of project scope and the messages being shared out to stakeholders.

Keep the balance. It's OK to assert your views and express the things you want to happen, as long as you keep the views and wants of others in mind.

Tips for improving practice

- Delegate ownership of actions and decisions as low as possible within the organisation structure of the team. Empower the team to find the best solution. Assertive leaders don't feel threatened by others making decisions.
- Practice speaking up for what you want and what the project needs. Rehearse difficult conversations before meeting with stakeholders. Write notes to remind you to bring up key points.
- Express your point with "I" language, for example:
  - □ I feel (strongly) that . . .
  - □ I would like to recommend . . .
  - □ I believe . . .
  - □ I will . . .
  - □ I chose/will choose to . . .
- Watch how others demonstrate assertive behaviour and learn from them.

Ethical awareness

The *APM Body of Knowledge* says:

> *Trust is gained by working consistently in a moral, legal and socially responsible manner.*

The framework for that responsible manner is ethics. Ethics is concerned with making the best possible decisions for the project, the environment and the people involved. Ethical practice is the result of:

- rules and regulations;
- values;
- codes of practice;
- rules and codes of conduct;
- moral principles.

Dealing with these ethical grey areas isn't an everyday occurrence for most project managers, but you should know what to do when something doesn't feel right.

Here are some examples of ethical issues in management that you might face:

- being asked to share confidential information;
- being asked to give more favourable consideration to one vendor in exchange for gifts or kickbacks;
- making hiring choices that are not purely influenced by who would be the best candidate for the job;
- being asked (or required) to give bribes in order to expedite work.

Generally, ethical issues come up when you're dealing with two individuals (or groups) that may have different agendas and expectations.

Tips for improving practice

- Disclose your personal and professional interests during negotiations and procurement discussions.
- Don't reuse intellectual property from previous employer in your current job.

- Avoid 'lying by omission'.
- Stand up for what you believe in.
- Call out unacceptable behaviour.
- Respectfully challenge where you believe the incorrect decision has been taken.
- Be respectful of your team's time e.g. don't expect them to do unpaid overtime.
- Treat everyone equally and don't show favouritism.

Action steps

- Pick a skill to work on during the coming month. Think about how you are going to develop that skill and how you can transition your new knowledge to the workplace to put it into practical use. Make a plan to do so.
- Put a note in your calendar for four weeks' time. This will be your reminder to assess your progress on building that skill. If you have achieved a level you are satisfied with, pick another skill to work on for the next four weeks.
- Ask your colleagues what they consider to be your core skills.
- Using the topics covered in this book, and your own ideas, complete a Stop, Start, Continue exercise. There is a template for this exercise in Appendix B. Consider the tasks you are doing to build a culture of engagement on your project. What do you need to stop doing? What do you need to start doing? What should you continue doing? Make notes for each of these so you can refer back to them.
- Put a reminder in your calendar to review your Stop, Start, Continue exercise in a month. Is it still valid? Refresh your actions to continually create a positive culture for engaging stakeholders.

Final words

If you've made it to the end of the book, you'll have a good understanding of the importance of applying a range of skills and techniques to the way you engage with stakeholders.

The previous chapters have provided a range of tips, tools and practical steps to help you improve the way you work with others.

To recap, everything we seek to do with engagement can be summed up in the formula:

UNDERSTANDING + ACTION + INFLUENCE = ENGAGEMENT

The point of engagement is to harness people power to improve project success.

It's worth reiterating that engagement is not an activity that happens in isolation, or because you choose to use one particular skill. Take a holistic, rounded view of the work you do with stakeholders. Stakeholder engagement touches many areas of project and business management from project prioritisation to succession planning, procurement to strategy development.

Remember that stakeholders aren't only involved with your project. Work across the programme or portfolio and with other project leaders to align your engagement activities where you can.

Despite your best efforts to apply some structure, engagement doesn't happen in a linear way. Sometimes it will feel like you can't plan the engagement, or it feels unnatural to try to 'engineer' a relationship with someone for the good of the project. When we work with people it can feel iterative, messy, uncoordinated, rushed and stressful.

Try not to worry. Even if it feels awkward for you, your stakeholders will see someone who cares about their views, wants the best for the organisation and the project and who is trying hard to make a positive difference.

Finally, remember that you and the project's stakeholders are people first, and project resources second (or even third, fourth, fifth or more). We all have good days and bad days; be kind to each other.

Engaging stakeholders on projects

No matter what your current level of experience with stakeholder engagement, there is always more to learn. In the pages that follow you'll find additional tools and information sources to help you take your professional development further in this area.

Appendix A provides a sample list of typical project stakeholders, as a jumping off point for your own stakeholder identification exercises.

Appendix B is the Stop, Start, Continue exercise to help you reflect on your current behaviours and plan for small improvements in the way you engage with others.

Appendix C contains case studies collated by the Association for Project Management Stakeholder Engagement Focus Group. They provide practical examples of what engagement looks like in real life.

The appendices are followed by references referred to in the book and useful further reading in book form and online via recommended websites.

Appendix A:
Stakeholder segments

This list is a starting point for you to consider the different individuals and stakeholder groups who could be stakeholders on your own project, programme or portfolio. Use the list as a tool for brainstorming and part of your stakeholder identification exercises.

- Internal teams:
  - Project team including project manager
  - Finance
  - IT: Change management, service transition, security
  - Business Analysis
  - Business change
  - Marketing/Digital
  - Sustainability, ethical practice, corporate social responsibility
  - Health and safety
  - Legal
  - Customer service
  - Sales/Commercial
  - Staff Groups/Unions
  - Procurement
  - HR
  - Other internal departments
- Customers:
  - Clients
  - Client/customer team members/end users
  - Customer managers
- Governance:
  - Project sponsor
  - Senior managers
  - Directors
  - PMO

Appendix A: Stakeholder segments

- Risk management
- Steering Group/Project Board
- Suppliers and partners
- Regulatory bodies
- The public
- Community groups
- Government agencies
- Shareholders

Your organisation may also consider the environment to be a stakeholder.

Appendix B: Stop, Start, Continue exercise

Stop, Start, Continue is an exercise in reflection. Use the headings to note down what activities you are going to stop doing, what you are going to start doing and what you will continue doing.

Keep a note of your answers and put time in your calendar to review your responses in a month's time. Did you stick to what you said you would do? What do you want to stop, start and continue to do now?

Stop, Start, Continue
Date:
What's working for you right now? What's not? Take a moment to reflect on how the month has been and how next month can build on this (or be different).
Stop: What are you going to stop doing?
Start: What are you going to start doing?
Continue: What are you going to continue doing?

Appendix C: Case studies

These case studies appear courtesy of the Association for Project Management Stakeholder Engagement Focus Group, whose members researched and curated them as part of the stakeholder resources available on the APM website.

Case study: Expansion of a university research facility

The university operated from a constrained urban site, with both historic and modern departmental buildings. In order to accommodate the footprint of the new graduate centre, the university had little choice but to demolish two existing structures in the heart of their campus and build higher and wider in their place.

Serious risks threatened the viability of this approach – the possibility of ground and nuclear laboratory contamination, a London Underground tube line directly beneath the proposed footprint, complex and unmapped services in the immediate area, and a historic graveyard nearby. The risks also came from within the institution itself, via business critical operations such as scheduled examinations, public events and externally funded research laboratories requiring stable and consistent conditions.

In order to mitigate these risks, stakeholder engagement was fundamental throughout the project, with risk workshops used to identify potential hazards and the vulnerability of the project to them. This was then followed up by subsidiary consultations with key stakeholders with knowledge in the areas of risk to be able to establish means to minimise the risk levels during the project.

Crucially this strategy was continuous and not merely a snapshot of risks at the time.

This approach of thorough and continual stakeholder engagement allowed the institution to be responsive to project changes, systematic and structured. It also allowed stakeholders to become part of the decision-making process, and ultimately created value – the gain through intelligent preparation outweighing the pain of the implementation process.

On potentially hazardous and difficult to manage operations, extensive stakeholder engagement of both general and risk specialised stakeholders allows risk mitigation and an improved decision-making process. These benefits, for the final project outcome, and the reduction of delays or risk related incidents is worth the initial effort to conduct the engagement process.

Case study: International research and development project

This case study recounts an international project that fared badly, mainly due to poor control of subcontractors (who are nonetheless stakeholders). There were other contributory factors including lack of risk management and false economy at the business case stage. The solution to the issues wiped out the anticipated project profit, and led to overall poor business performance, for both the primary organisation and its subcontractors.

A UK company ('Company X') was appointed to execute a prestigious research project on behalf of an overseas government, via a contract let by a (funded agency) organisation acting for that overseas government. This organisation is 'the customer'.

The project called for a significant amount of equipment to be built, commissioned and operated to some demanding standards.

As part of the business case, the costs of doing the work were researched and subdivided between various subcontractors, who would do the following:

- Build part of the equipment and all the control and instrumentation system, in the UK. This is Subcontractor A.
- Build the remainder of the equipment (which would need to interface with the equipment from Subcontractor A). This part of the equipment is being built overseas (not the customer's country) by a separate subcontractor (Subcontractor B).
- Assemble and operate the equipment at a site in yet another overseas country, operated by another subcontractor (Subcontractor C).

The project sponsor was the overseas sales manager of Company X, who gathered the information on costs from some of the key staff in the UK, and then presented the business case to the managing director of Company X, with whom agreement was reached that the costs and predicted profit margin were acceptable and that the project should proceed.

Once a contract had been agreed, the project sponsor brought in a project manager to oversee the day to day running of the project. The project manager had no involvement in the business case preparation, nor was any risk assessment done as part of the business case.

Subcontractor A had frequent churn of staff, unbeknown to the staff of Company X. Not long after letting the subcontract and the start of work, the key individual in Subcontractor A, who had been the primary point of contact in agreeing the specification and price, parted ways with Subcontractor A. His replacement was not technically conversant with the project as a whole.

The project manager from Company X also inherited a situation where the policing of some of the subcontracts was already earmarked to some of the key individuals who had been involved in the preparation of the business case. However, they were overloaded, and delegated to other project engineers in their department, outside the management authority of the project manager.

Progress reports from those project engineers were at first very promising but soon issues began to arise that the equipment, as-built, was not performing correctly. The new technical lead at Subcontractor A had not really grasped some of the key requirements but was not able to admit it, insisting that progress had just "hit a few snags".

Meanwhile, Subcontractors B and C were getting on with their tasks, making other pieces of equipment and preparing to operate the equipment. The date came for shipping Subcontractor A's product overseas, to Subcontractor C's site. The system, in particular the control and instrumentation system, wasn't ready. The control software programming was taking far longer than planned.

Eventually, a month late and after a heroic effort, the shipment was made.

Meanwhile, Subcontractor B had been busy and their equipment was sent to Subcontractor C pretty much on schedule. The real problems came when the equipment from A and B were coupled together and integration was attempted. This didn't work and a project engineer from Company X spent many fruitless weeks overseas, at Subcontractor C's site trying and failing to make the system work.

Weeks stretched into months and further faults were found: Subcontractor A hadn't been very fussy about cleanliness in their commissioning bay in the factory and their equipment was hopelessly contaminated with dirt, dust and grease. This affected the running of the plant and added more weeks to the commissioning, trying to clean and purge this system. The project manager was running out of goodwill from the customer, although the sponsor was kept fully aware and was highly supportive of all the efforts being made.

Things came to a head when the delays reached "unacceptable" and several months in magnitude.

The project manager was faced with a need to turn around a project which was drifting, partly because of the way it had been set up and partly because of factors beyond Company X's control. Everyone wanted to see rapid progress but to date it had been painfully slow due to technical issues. The challenge to the project manager was to assert full control over the project and to force change on both governance and technical fronts.

At significant cost, Company X and Subcontractor A agreed to send a joint team out to Subcontractor C. They spent around three weeks at Subcontractor C's site working seven day weeks and eventually turned the situation round. The control and implementation system was reprogrammed to include an interface with Subcontractor B's equipment. It eventually worked and the plant was cleaned up. However, this additional effort took most of the profit margin out of the contract, which lost all of its appeal to the business MD, the project found itself a 'lame duck' with little enthusiasm for it at board level.

Subcontractor A made a clear loss on their involvement in the project.

Despite having lost most of its profit margin on this contract, the benefit to Company X was avoidance of serious 'loss of reputation'. Further issues came to light later indicating that the specification of what Subcontractor B had to supply was inadequate, and some of that part of the equipment failed in service, at an early stage. That had to be remedied by a separate exercise, again at significant cost to Company X. The whole exercise ended with a significant financial loss, under some threat of legal action from the customer.

Company X no longer trades in the UK.

This was a project with a complex set of stakeholder interactions. Whilst communications were good overall and all parties were kept informed, there were times when the project manager was under pressure to delay a 'bad news' message, since the project engineer or subcontractor was sure "success lay just around the corner". There were a number of points where things could have been better. For example:

- No involvement of the project manager at bid and business case stage.
- Development of a risk register and its update through the business case and bid process, leading to a true appreciation of risk when the contract was agreed.

- Stronger policing of subcontractors even though key staff were overloaded.
- Lack of liability clauses in the subcontracts.
- Failure to recognise that subcontractors (who are stakeholders) need to be managed with a view that they may fail to complete their part of the project.

The experience provided a stern test to the project manager and his team and the episode is still referred to in the 'folklore' of the relevant industry.

Case study: Communication improvements in a hostel development project

This was a project to develop a hostel for the homeless in central London with strong local opposition.

The redevelopment scheme focused on redeveloping a derelict former nursing home into a hostel for homeless people. The charitable foundation behind the plan had identified a substantial need in the vicinity and had the backing of the local area's social services and support groups.

The building was a viable option due to the comparatively easy and cost-effective refurbishment relative to other options.

The main issue was the local resident opposition to the proposed plans which posed a real risk of planning permission refusal due to the lobbying group and extent of local concerns.

Due to the established need for the facility in the area and the financial incentive to redevelop this site as opposed to others, these local concerns would have to be heard and steps taken to resolve the problems to allow the renovation.

A series of stakeholder meetings were held, initially with all residents, in order to understand views and to explain the exact nature of the accommodation being provided. In parallel to the ongoing general stakeholder meetings that continued throughout the scheme, a smaller 'elected' group of residents formed and met with the foundation. These more strategic stakeholder meetings were the key to unlocking an informed dialogue which led to amendments to the scheme, including the introduction of a café run by residents.

These revisions were sufficient to satisfy some residents to a point where planning authorities were able to grant planning permission; a fundamental step for the project which was in real jeopardy without an effective stakeholder engagement programme.

Appendix C: Case studies

In conclusion, it became clear that both a general and a specialised stakeholder engagement programme were necessary to address such a locally contentious issue as the hostel development. Such an extensive outlook and willingness to compromise (for example, with the decision to include the café facilities) could be useful again in the future for other projects for which there is strong local opposition.

Notes and references

Association for Project Management 10 Principles of stakeholder engagement https://www.apm.org.uk/resources/find-a-resource/stakeholder-engagement/key-principles/

Association for Project Management Body of Knowledge, 7th Edition (2019). Princes Risborough: APM.

Association for Project Management Emerging Trends: Introduction to Gamification (2014). Princes Risborough: APM. Last accessed 10/3/20: https://www.apm.org.uk/sites/default/files/gamification%20-%20epdf.pdf

Berger, J. (2020) *The Catalyst: How to Change Anyone's Mind*. London: Simon & Schuster.

Blenko, M. W., Mankins, M. C. and Rogers, P. (2010) *Decide & Deliver: 5 Steps to Breakthrough Performance in Your Organization*. Boston: Harvard Business Review Press.

Crocker, A., Cross, R. and Gardner, H. K. (2018) 'How to make sure agile teams can work together', *Harvard Business Review*, May 15, 2018.

Ellis, C. D. (2020) *Culture Fix: How to Create a Great Place to Work*. Melbourne: Wiley.

Goldstein, N. J., Martin, S. J. and Cialdini, R. B. (2007) *Yes! 50 Secrets From the Science of* Persuasion. London: Profile Books.

Holloway, J., Bryde, D. and Joby, R. (2016) *A Practical Guide to Dealing with Difficult Stakeholders*. Abingdon: Routledge.

Jones, P. M. (2017) *Exactly What To Say: The Magic Words for Influence and Impact*. Vancouver: Page Two Books.

Kelman, H. C. (1958) 'Compliance, Identification, and Internalization: Three Processes of Attitude Change', *Journal of Conflict Resolution*. Vol. 2 (1) pp.51–60. Last accessed 11/2/20: https://scholar.harvard.edu/files/hckelman/files/Compliance_identification_and_internalization.pdf.

Marshall, C. (2018) *Technical Writing for Business People*. Swindon: BCS Learning & Development.

Martin, N. A. (2016) *Project Politics: A Systematic Approach to Managing Complex Relationships*. Abingdon: Routledge.

Notes and references

Mersino, A. (2013) *Emotional Intelligence for Project Managers, Second edition*. New York: AMACOM.

Mitchell, R. K., Agle, B. R. and Wood, D. J. (1997) 'Toward a Theory of Stakeholder Identification and Salience: Defining the Principle of Who and What Really Counts', *The Academy of Management Review*, Vol. 22 (4), pp. 853–886. Last accessed 10/3/20: http://www.jstor.org/stable/259247.

Pilkinton, A. (2020) 'Communications shape reality' in Phillips, M. (ed) (2020) *The Practitioner's Handbook of Project Performance: Agile, Waterfall and Beyond*, pp. 100–112. Abingdon: Routledge.

Rezvani, A. and Khosravi, P. (2020) 'Critical success and failure factors in large-scale complex projects' in Phillips, M. (ed) (2020) *The Practitioner's Handbook of Project Performance: Agile, Waterfall and Beyond*, pp. 100–112. Abingdon: Routledge.

Sapir, J. (2020) *Thriving at the Edge of Chaos: Managing Projects as Complex Adaptive Systems*. New York: Routledge/Productivity Press.

Settle-Murphy, N. (2013) *Leading Effective Virtual Teams*. Abingdon: Routledge.

Simon, P. (2015) *Message Not Received: Why Business Communication is Broken and How to Fix It*. Hoboken, NJ: Wiley.

Taleb, N. (2013) *Antifragile: Things That Gain From Disorder*. London: Penguin.

Wasson, K. (2020) *The Socially Intelligent Project Manager: Soft Skills That Prevent Hard Days*. Oakland: Berrett-Koehler.

We are grateful to the following for permission to reproduce copyright material:

Two figures adapted from 'Toward a Theory of Stakeholder Identification and Salience: Defining the Principle of Who and What Really Counts' by Ronald K. Mitchell, Bradley R. Agle and Donna J. Wood, *The Academy of Management Review*, Vol. 22 (4), 1997, pp.853–886. Reproduced by permission of Academy of Management via Copyright Clearance Center; Extracts from *Emotional Intelligence for Project Managers, Second edition* by Anthony Mersino, AMACOM, copyright © 2013. Reproduced by permission of HarperCollins Christian Publishing; 'Conflict Situations' based on Dr Ralph Kilmann's version of the TKI Conflict Model, copyright © 2009–2020 by Kilmann Diagnostics. All rights reserved. Original figure is available at: http://www.kilmanndiagnostics. com/overview-thomas-kilmann-conflict-mode-instrument-tki; and 'Engagement modes' adapted from *Practical People Engagement: Leading Change through the Power of Relationships* by Patrick Mayfield, Elbereth Publishing, 2013. Reproduced by permission of Patrick Mayfield.

Bibliography

This is a list of recommended resources for further reading.

General stakeholder engagement

Bourne, L. (2011) *Advising Upwards: A Framework for Understanding and Engaging Senior Management Stakeholders*. Farnham: Gower.

Bourne, L. (2016) *Stakeholder Relationship Management: A Maturity Model for Organisational Implementation*. Abingdon: Routledge.

Harrin, E. and Peplow, P. (2012) *Customer-Centric Project Management*, Farnham: Ashgate.

Kawasaki, G. (2011) *Enchantment: The Art of Changing Hearts, Minds, and Actions*. London: Penguin.

Mayfield, P. (2013) *Practical People Engagement: Leading Change through the Power of Relationships*. Abingdon: Elbereth Publishing.

Worsley, L. (2017) *Stakeholder-Led Project Management: Changing the Way we Manage Projects*. New York: Business Expert Press.

Project communication

Harrin, E. (2017) *Communicating Change: How to Talk About Project Change*. London: Bookboon.

Patterson, K., Grenny, J., McMillan, R. and Switzler, A. (2011) *Crucial Conversations: Tools for Talking When Stakes Are High, Second Edition*. New York: McGraw-Hill.

Taylor, P. (2014) *Project Branding: Using Marketing to Win the Hearts and Minds of Stakeholders*. Minnetonka: RMC Publications, Inc.

Theobald, T. and Cooper, C. (2012) *Shut up and listen: Communication with impact*. Basingstoke: Palgrave Macmillan.

Bibliography

Meetings

Kaner, S. (2014) *Facilitator's Guide to Participatory Decision-Making, Third Edition*. San Francisco: Jossey-Bass.

Maltzman, R. and Stewart, J. (2018) *How to Facilitate Productive Project Planning Meetings: A Practical Guide to Ensuring Project Success*. New Jersey: Maven House.

Pullan, P. and Murray-Webster, R. (2016) *A Short Guide to Facilitating Risk Management: Engaging People to Identify, Own and Manage Risk*. Abingdon: Routledge.

Social networks

Cross, R. and Parker, A. (2004) *The Hidden Power of Social Networks: Understanding How Work Really Gets Done in Organisations*. Boston: Harvard Business School Publishing.

Scott, J. (2017) *Social Network Analysis, Fourth Edition*. London: SAGE Publications.

Conflict management

Blake, S., Browne, J. and Sime, S. (2018) *A Practical Approach to Alternative Dispute Resolution, Fifth Edition*. Oxford: Oxford University Press.

Cornelius, H. and Faire, S. (2014) *Everyone Can Win: Responding to Conflict Constructively, Second Edition*. Chatswood: Simon & Schuster.

Shearouse, S. H. (2011) *Conflict 101: A manager's guide to resolving problems so everyone can get back to work*. New York: AMACOM.

Useful websites

apm.org.uk/about-us/how-apm-is-run/apm-code-of-professional-conduct
The APM website also includes the Code of Professional Conduct for an overview of ethical standards in project management and expected professional behaviour.

apm.org.uk/resources/find-a-resource/stakeholder-engagement
The APM website has a useful resource page on stakeholder engagement, curated by the Stakeholder Engagement Focus Group. The group shares a regular round up of stakeholder engagement resources and news.

energybartools.com
The Energy Bar Tools website from Rick Maurer shares a free 'energy bar' resource to enable you to visualise the journey stakeholders need to go through to reach the level of engagement you require from them. It includes other useful articles etc. on change management and reducing resistance to change.

girlsguidetopm.com
A Girl's Guide To Project Management is one of the longest-running project management blogs and has a wealth of free resources, project management templates, articles and interviews curated by this book's author, Elizabeth Harrin.

kilmanndiagnostics.com
Kilmann Diagnostics is a site from Dr Ralph H. Kilmann and includes lots of useful information and resources relating to conflict management.

praxisframework.org
The Praxis Framework is a freely accessible framework for managing projects, programmes and portfolio. It includes a knowledgebase of resources along with a methodology and other resources.

Index

Index

Index

More books from Elizabeth Harrin

Shortcuts to success: project management in the real world
BCS, 2013

Anything from an office move to the Olympic Games can be termed a project but it takes time to gain the experience required to be confident on the job. Not any more: this book contains the wisdom of project managers totalling over 250 years of professional project management experience in a highly accessible format. This practical and entertaining book will help project managers get up to speed quickly with good practice, avoid pitfalls and deliver business value.

> "Packed with hard-won insights on how to make projects work in today's pressurised business environment. Apply what it suggests and you're likely to save your company a fortune and yourself heaps of frustration!"
>
> *Dr Penny Pullan, Director, Making Projects Work Ltd.*

Customer-centric project management *Routledge, 2012.*
Co-authored with Phil Peplow

There has been a sea-change in the focus of organisations away from a traditional product or service centricity towards customer-centricity – and projects are just as much a part of that change.

Projects must deliver value and the authors demonstrate convincingly that stakeholders are the ones who get to decide what 'value' actually means.

This short guide explains the importance of customer-centricity to project performance and demonstrates the tools and processes to guide customer-centric thinking in your project teams. The book provides a straightforward implementation guide to delivering engagement, even on difficult projects.

> "[This approach] allowed us to achieve fantastic results in terms of customer satisfaction. It enabled us to channel our energies into precisely what our customers were looking for – a consistently excellent service."
>
> *Neil Harrison, CEO, Travelex*

More Books From Elizabeth Harrin

Collaboration tools for project managers *PMI, 2016*

Today's project leaders face the challenge of managing projects effectively using tested and reliable methods, while also trying out the new methods preferred by some global and tech-savvy team members and stakeholders.

Information travels faster than ever before. Project teams are called upon to produce relevant and up-to-date project information, increase productivity and deliver results through top-notch communications.

Social media and online communications tools have rapidly changed our world outside the workplace. These platforms and other tools like wikis and big data repositories offer exciting possibilities to improve project team collaboration and stakeholder communication in the workplace as well.

Since project managers rely on communication and effective team management skills, they need to keep up with the fast pace of change, technology trends and the latest business drivers that help move organisations forward.

This book builds on Elizabeth's 2010 book, *Social Media for Project Managers* and is fully updated. It provides the latest information, success stories and an easy-to-follow guide to implementing online collaboration tools successfully.

It's time for project teams to explore how online collaboration tools can help them to communicate faster, work virtually with people across the globe and get better business results.

> "As project managers, we can no longer just manage our project details; schedule, budget, quality, scope. Yes, they do need to be managed, but it is becoming much more than that. One must, as Elizabeth says "create collaborative environments where people can do their best work . . ." That environment will not only make the project manager more effective, but will make the project more successful, something we all strive for. In her book, *Collaboration Tools for Project Managers*, Elizabeth does just that; help the project manager use all the collaborative tools available. She defines the tools, provides the reasoning behind their effectiveness, and how to use them for their maximum value. Elizabeth also provides a roadmap to a myriad of resources as well as inviting the reader into the conversation. This book is a must read for all project managers who want to be more effective, and I believe that is what we all want."
>
> *David Shirley, PMP, author, educator, and Cleland Project Management Literature Award Winner*